Some critical praise ... 's
Voice Left . . .

"Dom van Zeller is already well known for his popular classics
on spiritual subjects . . . he writes on subjects in this volume
that might of special interest to the busy man: self-pity, experience, humility and reticence, responsibility, restlessness
and contemplation . . ." *The Catholic World*

"Those who like their spiritual food liberally seasoned with
wit and common sense will find him the man for them."
Ave Maria

"The author deserves a special accolade for his consistent
freshness of style and his compact presentation of profound
truths on the supernatural life for laymen . . . Has all the
appealing qualities of the previous works." *America*

Other Image Books by Dom Hubert van Zeller . . .

We Work while the Light Lasts: "Whenever and wherever
Father van Zeller's pen strikes paper, sparks fly up and a light
is kindled." Msgr. John S. Kennedy
Catholic Transcript

We Die Standing Up: "Before us are laid the simple, profound, most difficult demands we must inevitably make upon
ourselves in desiring and achieving real love of God and
man." *Integrity*

We Live with Our Eyes Open: "Good spiritual reading
. . . highly personal 'catchy' style." *Catholic World*

DATE DUE

IDEAL 3370 UNGUMMED, 3371 GUMMED   PRINTED IN U.S.A.

WE SING WHILE THERE'S VOICE LEFT

DOM HUBERT VAN ZELLER, O.S.B.

*I will proclaim Thy renown to my brethren;
where Thy people gather, I will join in singing Thy praises.*

PSALM XXI, 23

*Life will bring you many misfortunes, but you
will be happy on account of them. You will
bless life and cause others to bless it.*

DOSTOIEVSKI

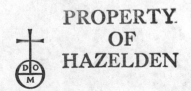
IMAGE BOOKS
A Division of Doubleday & Company, Inc.
Garden City, New York

Image Books Edition 1964
by special arrangement with Sheed & Ward, Inc.
Image Books Edition published September, 1964

Printed in the United States of America

For
Brian Whitlock and Christopher Hull
who will recognise bits of this book—
though not, I add hastily, the same bits.

CONTENTS

INTRODUCTION

Critics tell me that the world, life, problems of relationship between God and man are not so clear-cut as I seem to make them. "It isn't simply a question of right and wrong," I am reminded; "black is never wholly black, nor white wholly white. There must always be a good deal of grey." Certainly, but if you look at the space in between, you begin to *see* grey. The point about books like this is that you are invited to break up the all too prevalent grey into its component black and white. Man can so easily fool himself about the grey. Where in earlier books of the present sequence it was the darker side of the world, of life, of human relationship that was mostly discussed, in this one it is chiefly the lighter and more hopeful.

Presumably it is the purpose of every ideology to save the world. Unless you know both what you are saving it from and what you are saving it for, the process will not get you very far. The Christian ideology is clear on both points: the world is being saved from itself and for God. It is the absurdly ambitious aim of this book to help in the operation. Few would deny that the world has moved very fast and very far in the last ten years; the question is, however, whether it has moved in the right direction. Fear of missing the train and being left on the platform has blinded us—yes, us Catholics—to the fact that the train may be going the wrong way. It is no good having a ticket on the train, knowing all about the train, enjoying one's journey in the train, favourably comparing the time and the upholstery and the view out of the window with other trains, *if* one fails to reach one's destination. It is better to miss the right train than to catch the wrong one—in the same way that it is better to back the wrong horse than to *be* the wrong horse—because at least the situation can be remedied. The whole matter is what the soul is going *towards*. The present essays do not make up a spiritual Bradshaw, but they do attempt to show the over-confident as well as the hesitant traveller how to read the signals. If there are accidents on the line it won't be my fault.

Two of the chapters in this book have appeared in *The Key*, to the editor of which I express my thanks for allowing me to include them here, and the sequence on Communism represents the substance of a course delivered on this subject to the Oratory School. In reading about Communism I made notes from a number of sources, but since I had then no thought of publication I am afraid I did not bother to specify names. The only authority whom I can remember is Mr. Hyde, of whose excellent writings I certainly made a study, and to him, as to any other whose work is reflected in these pages, I tender most grateful acknowledgements.

WE SING WHILE THERE'S VOICE LEFT

WHAT RELIGION DOES FOR US

There are some propositions of religion to which a mere notional assent is not enough. To get any good out of them at all we must take them to bits and put them together again in such a way that they mean something to us. Perhaps the first of such propositions is the truth that God, quite simply, loves us. He had no need to create us, but, having created us, He loves us. Indeed it is because of that love that we are alive at all. It is as impossible for Him not to love us as it is for Him not to love Himself. But whereas He loves Himself because He is all good and therefore the perfect object of love, He loves us in spite of the fact that we are nowhere near all goodness and are far from being perfect objects of love. He loves us because He is good, not because we are. We may behave abominably and reject His love. We may forget that He has any claim upon us. We may choose to cross the line and go over to His enemies. But His love is always there, waiting. The knowledge of this is perhaps the most elemental, as well as the most necessary, gift to man. If our religion can really convince us that we are the personal objects of God's love, it has provided us with a scheme into which everything else can be made to fit.

Always at the back of our minds there is the thought: "Why should God love me? I am on such an entirely different plane, and in any case am not in the least likely to give Him what He wants." Surely the answer to this is not to look at our side of the relationship at all, but at His. Once we allow that God is love, once we accept the fact that He is what we conceive to be goodness itself, it should not be difficult to go on from there and admit—if even from our own experience of human goodness—that perfection tends to communicate itself. Goodness, love, truth—those qualities which we see reflected in the world around us—have a way of imparting themselves in the measure to which they are possessed. If God possesses them perfectly, He must want to communicate them perfectly. If there is any obstacle to the complete and intimate reception of His gifts, the obstacle must be on our side. *De ratione boni est,* says St. Thomas, *quod se aliis communicet.* We, like Him, should be there— waiting. It is this which our religion should be teaching us to do: we ought, if the work of religion is operating properly within us, to be growing more and more receptive, more and more ready to respond.

Granted, then, that God loves us. What next? "Oh yes, I know—the Passion. He has redeemed us by His Precious Blood. Also He has put heaven within our reach. I know all this. But it seems so remote and impersonal. I believe it, but it isn't a living reality to me. I want to be aware of God's love in the way that I am aware of a person's love. I want to be able to see it as I can see it in a person's eyes, and know it as I can know that it is going on in another's heart even when I am miles away and thinking of something else." In other words you want not to believe it but to taste it. You want to have the experience of it. You do not want religion at all, but the feeling of it. You are back at your side of the relationship, not at God's.

Religion, to repeat, is our means of responding. Nowhere are we told that it is our means of experiencing. The enjoyment is the reward; the experience is the ultimate, and not necessarily the present, goal. Religion shows us the way. It even carries us along the way. But we do not take it up for the sake of being carried.

"To love anything", says St. Thomas, "is to will good to that thing." It is nothing other than this. If love considers more the good which can be got out of the thing loved than the good which may come to it, it is no true love. God's love for us is true love itself, and our good is therefore His will. He wants what is best for us *all the time.* His will never ceases the act of providing for us the means of happiness and holiness. Each one of us is a distinct and individual object of His creation, redemption, conservation, and plan for eternal destiny. There should not be anything remote or impersonal about this. Certainly there should be no thought of His loving us for anything in the way of service which He can get out of us. Even when we have done all that we can to please Him we are unprofitable servants. And there cannot be many of us who do all that we can to please Him. We say we have done our best, but in our hearts we know that we have not. If God were loving us for what we had to give, He would be dooming Himself to disappointment.

To sum up. Religion gives us God's love. Without any merit of ours, religion provides us with a claim upon all that is needed to make a success of this life, and, so long as we make use of what is provided, there is the absolute promise of happiness in the life to come. Religion gives us assurance of truth, direction and purpose in our struggle towards light, hope in an ultimate satisfaction of our desire. What religion does not give—and it is this that we are always expecting it to give—is the guarantee that we shall enjoy thrills and be uninterruptedly conscious of the truth of its every implication. To ask from religion, which is nothing else but divine love extended in two directions, the same emotions as are looked for in reciprocated human love is to mistake the mode of its expression. The terms of the relationship are defined by God and not by man. All that man has to do is to trust, and hope, and love back.

WHAT WE DO FOR RELIGION

We can, if we are bent on it, do nothing. God gives us the power of making no contribution whatever. He leaves us absolutely free. If, on the other hand, we decide to respond and take our souls seriously—or rather if we decide to take His Gospel seriously—there open out immediately an infinite number of degrees of possible service. The first thing we can do is to obey His laws. "If you love Me keep My commandments"; the answer to the first of the rich young man's questions was perfectly clear. How can there be any other way of showing that we understand the implications of religion? But we are not bound to stop short at giving our submission to the laws of God and Church: we can go on to give ourselves. Much will be said about the necessity of falling in with the order, natural and supernatural, established by God. For the moment, however, we are considering not so much what we *must* do, but what we *can* do, for God. And again, as in the foregoing section, the approach is rather to look at the matter from God's angle than from ours.

God wants the whole of us. Not a piece of our personality, but the whole. He wants all that He has given us—which is everything. That is why He gave it. St. Augustine says that we have been given free will so that we might freely give back our wills to Him. If God had wanted less from us, He would not have given so much.

"But this is terribly cramping!" we cry at once; "I'm apparently expected to surrender not only my desires when they run contrary to my conscience—and this, after all, is reasonable enough—but also my individuality. Where is it going to stop? Is God going to demand my time, my thoughts, my way of judging things, my ambitions? Am I to have nothing under my own control? If such is the case, I might just as well be a machine." The idea of surrendering to God is, if it is not a welcome challenge to our generosity, a cause of bewilderment and often a definite stumbling-block. We can understand a religious renouncing the right to possess property, and we can see that the best thing for the sick or the aged or the afflicted is to loosen their hold on what is being taken from them; but we imagine that without either a special call from God or the inescapable force of circumstance, the surrender of self is not expected. "I refuse to let go of my personality," we say, "because if I do there will be nothing left." Let this statement be examined.

When someone gives his whole self, body and soul, to God —and this should be nothing out-of-the-way—there is no impoverishment of personality. In fact the individuality is enriched. When a soul is deliberately handed over to God, it receives something infinitely more worth while than what was felt to be specifically its own before. God does not scoop something out of the soul and leave it empty; He puts something into it, and develops its very essence. What has happened is that the life of grace is now at last being given a chance. Real life has begun. You would not say that the seed was losing anything in becoming a plant or that the candle was being frustrated by being lit. Once the soul, against its instinctive desire to strike out its own line of independence, is made over to God—in other words once the rebellion left behind by original sin is repudiated—it acquires a new perfection to its identity. By realising its place in God, it realises itself. A soul might certainly be said to miss something of its God-given identity if it were slavishly to follow the memory of a saint—because for one thing we tend to model ourselves upon the less significant aspects of our heroes' example, and for another we can't be sure that this particular interpretation of sanctity is what is required of *us*—but there can be no possible loss in giving over the reins to Wisdom Itself.

The first condition of holiness and security in the practice of religion, then, is to take our Lord's words literally and worship with our *whole* heart. Nothing kept from Him, nowhere to which He may not come, not a person or a hope or an interest which is not equally His. Even our weaknesses, our secret concessions to self, our excuses are—though they cannot be shared by Him—at least confided to the care of God. It is not only our sins that He must know about: He must be admitted to our follies as well. What keeps us back from so absolute a commitment? Partly ignorance of the true situation and its possibilities, partly laziness, mostly fear. It is the absurd fear of being put upon. We think we shall be cheated. "God will take more than we bargained for." He may do, and probably will; but we shall be vastly better off if He does. If the seed could refuse to grow, it probably would. The earthiness of its environment would urge the disadvantages of fresh air. If the candle could decide against being lit, it probably would. The drawbacks to being burned are obvious. But we *have* to grow, we *have* to face the flame.

There is no loss in giving to God and to religion; there can only be gain.

An artist once said to me when there was a question of his becoming a Catholic: "I know that if I once join your Church I shall have to do without myself. It would kill my art. I can't do it." He was quite wrong of course—at all events about it killing his art—but one saw what he meant. Self has to be handed over. What happens then is the hundredfold return. But people do not see further than the renunciation of self and so remain embedded—in self. And incidentally if my artist friend had been able to make the act of surrender he would not now have to face the fact that his painting has quite obviously come to a dead end.

JOY—OF A SORT

The joy which will be considered here is not the mellow, quiet, comfortable joy which is better thought of as contentment. It is not, that is to say, the kind of pleasure which comes from books, or watching cricket, or sitting in front of a fire with a dog on one's knees and nothing to think about but heaven and the next meal, or from a May morning by a trout stream when the sun is just beginning to play games on the surface of the water and there is the sound of a horse neighing in the distance. These joys are real, but they are not the sort we have in mind. The joy which we have now to examine—and then to compare with others somewhat higher in the scale—has no serenity about it: it is the one which is included by theologians among the "minor passions". This kind makes all the others (such as those instanced above) seem tame and even boring. Which is exactly why we have to examine it. The simpler joys are *not* tame and boring—unless the exciting kind, by being overworked, make them so. The first thing, then, is to enquire into that fleeting mood of ecstasy which lifts us out of our setting in time, and gives us the illusion of everlasting bliss. When we have got that right, and put it in its place, we can turn back and look at the more tranquil and elemental pleasures of life —which in any case more or less run themselves.

At the outset it must be insisted that though an emotion may be labelled a "passion", it need not necessarily be something guilty. Our Lord Himself experienced joy, fear, and so on—only in His case these emotions are called "pro-passions" because there was no excess or clouding of the judgement. With us there is often both excess and clouding of the judgement: the minor passions can sweep us off our feet and land us on dangerous ground. The minor are all too closely related to the major, and can serve as an easy introduction.

The joy which robs us, even temporarily, of our balance comes to us mostly through the senses. It is not that the senses are wicked—any more than joy is wicked. It is simply that the combination of stimulated senses and receptive emotions leads as often as not to a wicked sort of enjoyment. When unguarded senses (or, to be accurate, when senses which are functioning according to their proper nature but which are providing more material than is good for the natural appetite) are found to be co-operating with willing mental sensibilities, there results a recklessness which it becomes extraordinarily hard for the will to control. The excitement which is stirred up by all this is more than just a spasm of restlessness which can be soothed without either consent or denial: it is something which calls for making up one's mind. When nature is clamouring for a joy, even if it is a quite legitimate joy, it is in fact looking for a liberation of some sort. It wants to exercise the power of living in top gear. Inevitably this is a desire which has its dangers.

Man is meant to perceive things with the senses and enjoy what he perceives. Man is meant to live life to the full within the limits of God's law. What man is not meant to do is to confuse indulgence of the senses with the fullness of life. If he does this there is rebellion and chaos.

All sins (and this can be seen especially in all sense sins) are a snatching at a joy which is felt to be a good enough substitute for the real thing. Whether the senses are first in the field, proposing a certain satisfaction to the imagination, or whether the appetite starts the thing off by casting about for gratification among the senses, the result is the same: the will finds itself faced with a demand which is both sensual and emotional. Reason may point out that the proposed gratification is not worth it, is no solution, is a betrayal of purpose, is in the long run a flat contradiction of what the soul is going all out to claim. But where the excitement has boiled up, where the will has begun to wobble, there is no response to reason. Joy is demanded, possessed for a moment, seen through, and finally discarded for something else. But always there is the illusion of happiness, the believed—if un-formulated—anticipation of heaven.

Take any gratification you like. Take the obvious and gross one of drunkenness. To be absolutely without care, to feel the sense of complete freedom, to know that nothing matters—nothing. But all sin, while it lasts, is intoxicating. To control a power for evil, no less than to possess a person, lends an inside-out illusion of good. The reason why love can degenerate into passion, the reason why passion can get mixed up with love at all and hold its own, is simply because human beings can sense in each other that element of eternity for which their minds and bodies crave.

So much for the joy which, to say the least of it, rests on thin ice. But is there nothing between the heady joys of licence and the safer joys of library, pavilion, armchair, and trout-stream? Has the choice got to be between what is sinful and what is staid? "After all," it might be objected, "even your list of unexciting pleasures, worthy though the examples may be, fails in the essential. What we look for in our joys is some sort of guarantee of happiness. If the respectable pleasures are no more lasting than the reprehensible ones, it is a lot to ask that we should invariably opt for respectability." The answer is surely that there is exquisite joy to be found without having to resort to sin for it, and that such joy, though perhaps less delirious, is far more lasting. The joy of bringing up a family, for instance, or the joy of achievement after struggle. What about the joy of reciprocated affection?—not of reciprocated passion now, but affection? This may be less exhilarating than the other, but it is certainly not boring. What about the joys of discovery, of vindicated confidence, of hope, of devotion to a cause or a person or a principle? What about the joy of knowing that one's soul is in order, and that good is stronger than evil, love stronger than hate? There are a good many joys to which we may abandon ourselves without fear of being either bored or to blame or likely to be left next morning with a sense of emptiness and anti-climax. Christ came that we might have joy, and that our joy might be full. It is we, by not referring it back to Him, who empty it of its meaning. Taking it from Him with ready hands, refusing to hoard it or exploit it behind His back, grateful for the privilege of being admitted to it, we are not likely to be disappointed. His are better than the other kind, and by their fruits we shall know them. Though as a matter of fact we do not have to wait until they bear fruit: most of us know all about our joys before we have started pruning the branches. In our heart of hearts we acknowledge all along that there is one joy which responds to impulse and is as unsatisfying as the appetite is insatiable, and that there is another which is to be found in the things which make for peace—the peace "which the world cannot take from you."

IS SIN SO JOLLY?

There is a catch in most things, but in nothing so much as in sin. Suppose we assume—and the assumption needs no great effort of self-analysis—that the advantages which we feel we are getting out of sin are roughly these: excitement, the sense of escape from the ordinary, the illusion of satisfaction to mind and body, the feeling of being independent and in control. There are other minor joys to be found in committing sin, and to a large extent it depends upon what kind of sin you happen to be determined to commit, but in the main there is the idea of snatching at a piece of fun which with any luck will turn out to be really gratifying after all—and which in any case will be more pleasant than what is going on at the moment. All sin may *amount* to rebellion against God, but it is not always committed in terms of rebellion: more often it is seen simply as a likely substitute, as a means of getting away. The body hungers, the mind hopes, the safeguards fall away, and the reserves are spent in a moment. Sin.

We need not here go into the question of anti-climax and remorse. All we want to consider at the moment is the essential unsatisfactoriness of sin as a practice. Some people take much longer than others to realise the emptiness of the experiment: they are encouraged, like lucky gamblers, by their early successes. The devil sees to this. The novelty of it *does* give the desired sense of emancipation, of delirious pleasure, of mastery and ownership. This is precisely the danger—people imagine later on that such initial success can be kept up if they only go about it the right way. But the first thrill of sin cannot be reclaimed any more than the innocence of childhood can be enjoyed for ever. The sinner finds that he has to gear himself up to greater effort in order to gratify an appetite which in the beginning was fed with comparative ease. The satisfactions have to be both more frequent and more intense.

In the business of sowing wild oats there are some who are very soon brought to acknowledge the quality of the harvest. These are fortunate, for they immediately start looking round for better fields, for more durable sorts of fun, for a promise of a more satisfactory yield. But it is the others whom one is considering here—the sowers who are determined to be confident in next year's harvest. "The wild oats are worth it," they say: "expensive perhaps, but worth it." They think they can always go on getting fun; and even if at any given time the pleasure is found to pall or the price is felt to be rather more than was bargained for, there is always the expectation that with a change of mood or with a more careful selection or with a more subtle approach the old excitement can be re-lived, the old freedoms recaptured. It is this fatal belief that satisfaction is just round the corner, and that it is simply a matter of losing yourself in it when you have managed to get hold of it, that keeps people wasting their minds, their bodies, their energies, and their readiness to respond to grace *long after their sins have given them up.* People will sacrifice their friends, will go back on their memories and upbringing, will risk their careers and their health and their peace of mind—to say nothing of their immortal souls—in the absurd conviction that they can bring off a deal with sin. They will not come to terms with happiness; they think they can manage something better. Even when they *know* that this "something better" is a substitute, and that happiness is the commodity for which their souls are craving, they are often too proud to admit their mistake.

It requires courage and some humility to bring ourselves to the point of admitting that we have barked up the wrong tree for years when almost any fool could have seen a forest of right ones. The trouble is that we can go on climbing our wrong tree until we are too afraid to come down. Not always too comfortable to come down—because sin is not always comfortable—but too frightened. Frightened and obstinate. We fear the consequences of leaving sin for grace; we obstinately refuse to say that we have made fools of ourselves. So we stay where we are. And we sin.

To sum up. The sinner is blocked all along the line by the Law of Diminishing Returns. Each time he sins he gets less and less satisfaction out of it. This, however, is not the only drawback. A greater evil lies in the fact that each time he sins he sees himself more and more as identified with his sin. Here, indeed, is the supreme tragedy of the determined sinner—that his soul becomes set in opposition to the influence of grace. He is so used to finding a spurious happiness of body and mind in sin that he ceases to feel the urge to look for any other kind of happiness elsewhere. He is at home in evil; it is his element. He may know, either from the occasional twinges of his conscience or from the sight of a more real happiness in other people, that he is missing the only thing which is at all worth while, but so far as practi-

cal considerations go he is content to take his contentment
in his sin. "At least," the sinner tells himself, "I am my own
master. I am responsible to myself. I can make my own laws,
and break everybody else's." The delusion could hardly be
more complete: the man who is tied to his sin is far more
tightly bound than he could possibly be if he were obedient
to the laws which he happens to be breaking.

SELF-PITY

Such is the perversity of the human mind that a man will
prefer an unhappiness of his own choice to a happiness which
God is holding out to him. He makes himself at home in
his artificial world, the world which he has built up for himself at the cost of heaven knows what waste of God's will,
and does not want to be dislodged. In his heart he knows
that he is made for something more than the snug selfishness
of his cocoon existence, but he cannot bring himself to accept
the terms of the offer. He cannot, though acknowledging the
validity of God's promise, throw off his petty egoism and
greed.

This is why we prefer the idea of living on earth to the
idea of living in heaven: we admit that heaven is happiness,
but we like our kind of happiness better than God's. This is
also why we are prepared to go on heaping up for ourselves
our hell on earth: it is at least ours. We know that we have
no one to blame but ourselves for our misery. We hate
being miserable, but we feel we should be far more miserable
if we were not.

People imagine that self-pity is the same as canvassing for
sympathy. It is not. The real expert in self-pity has no need
of other people's commiseration: he can do it all himself. Indeed he has sufficient insight into the working of the human
mind to realise that the world would soon get tired of giving
him sympathy. He takes care not to be pitied for being pathetic. So he keeps as far as possible out of men's way. Which

forces him back upon himself and gives him further opportunity. Of all indulgences, that of secret self-pity is surely one of the most harmful. The secret drinker feels ashamed, the glutton feels the ache of satiety, the man whose passion carries him to excess feels a reaction against the pleasures which excited him; but the man who hugs his misery wants more and more . . . and there is no shame or remorse.

Why don't we see that our indulgence is sheer luxury, sheer waste? The truth is that we do see, but that we prefer to wallow and to spend ourselves uselessly. "Why should I look at reality," we say, "when I have got television?" It is the old story of substitutions: the choice of what is less worth while leading us so far down the scale of values that we end up by having neither the energy nor the desire to climb up again. The substance is refused, the shadows come to stay . . . Plato's cave-dwellers will not look beyond the wall. God offers a fact, and man takes refuge in a fake; it is man's own fault if he pities himself for the hardness of his lot. This is precisely the point—he *knows* the fault is his. Yet he goes on pitying and adding to the hardness.

There can be no remedy for this but to surrender into the hands of God. As it was the lust for independence which caused the trouble so it must be a return to submission which will get it right. Very little use to resolve not to complain, not to dwell deliberately upon the subject of one's afflictions: one must get at the cause as well as strangle the effects. The cause is simply self-will. Unless the will to be potentially pitiable is ruthlessly denied it is difficult to see how anything can be done.

One of the most subtle pieces of character-drawing in *The Pilgrim's Progress* is that which gives us Mr. Fearing, who, it will be remembered, "had a Slough of Despond in his mind; a slough that he carried everywhere with him or else he could never have been as he was." Mr. Great-heart gives an account of how his dejected companion responded to what they passed on the way to the Celestial City. "When we were come to where the three fellows were hanged, he said that such would, he feared, be his end also." At the

House Beautiful, which Mr. Fearing entered "before he was willing", he "desired much to be alone". Coming to the Valley of Humiliation, "he went down as well as ever I saw man in my life", and "when he was come to the entrance of the Valley of the Shadow of Death, I thought I should have lost my man". But even Mr. Fearing, with all his awareness of suffering and his reluctance to make the act of trust, was not beyond rescue in the end. To Mr. Honest's enquiry as to how the poor man fared in the finish, Great-heart says, "I never had doubt about him . . . he was a man of choice spirit, but always kept very low, and that made his life so burdensome to himself and so troublesome to others". Christiana's conclusions about Fearing are worth noting. "His troubles lay so hard upon him," she reflects, "that they made him so that he could not knock at the houses of entertainment. This relation of Mr. Fearing has done me much good. I thought there had been nobody like me." Precisely because there are so many of us like her there is reason to hope that we shall be able to climb out of our particular Sloughs of Despond.

EXPERIENCE

When St. Guthlac was hauled over the coals for being too tolerant with the noisy and often inconsiderate young people who flocked after him wherever he went, the only answer his critics received from the saint was that the fruits of age were not to be looked for in youth. Even the devils advanced the charge of over-gentleness. "It isn't a sin to be immature," said St. Guthlac, "and the longer my friends can retain their high spirits—even if rather boisterous at times—the better." In the end (though this is by the way) St. Guthlac was left alone both by those who had found fault with his treatment of the young and by the young themselves: the last fifteen years of his life were spent in solitude on the marshes. But even as a hermit he had a following—of wild fowl.

If experience blunts one edge, it sharpens another. Innocence, spontaneity, wonder, zest, and the generosity which is so uncalculating that it can come perilously close to a recklessness which is wrong—in fact all those qualities which we begin to appreciate and find attractive only when we have ourselves outgrown them—may be compensated for. Experience can, if we let it, give us something better than the happy accident of youth. People will tell you, with a wistful look in their eye, that the loss of their early idealism has never been made good by any of the advantages that have come to them in later life. Well, whose fault is that? Either they were sentimentalists in the first place and not true idealists at all, or else they allowed the world to rob them of what was theirs by right. The mere mounting up of years cannot—that is to say *need* not—affect the issue. The whole thing turns on what is made of experience.

Now though experience is, as spiritual writers are at pains to point out, one of the most costly as well as one of the most valuable helps to the soul, it can be rendered completely valueless if we refuse to go on paying for its upkeep. "A man, sir," said Dr. Johnson, "should keep his friendships in constant repair," and the same might be said of all other experience. By allowing our experience go stale on us, by imagining that life has taught us all we need to know, we harden into just that state of insensibility which it is the main purpose of experience to counteract. Experience is meant to give us insight into other people's ways of thinking; it is not intended to relieve us of having to think ourselves. Experience, however expensive it is to us personally, is not designed *solely* to provide us with poise, a habit of easy self-confidence, the respect of others, and a card-index mind. We come by it hardly, and sometimes bitterly, because we would never learn its lesson if it were handed to us on a plate. But it is not intended to be for our benefit and nobody else's.

Designed primarily to assist the gift of understanding, experience can produce exactly the opposite result and positively block the impact of mind upon mind. The kind of experience which makes a man cynical, case-hardened, indifferent to the claims of what had moved him in the days of his narrower knowledge is obviously not going to make for sympathy. Better not to have had the knowledge at all. Better to have stopped on in a fools' paradise where at least he would have had the company of other fools—than to find himself cast out of paradise with no kindred spirits but knaves.

Experience is like learning: it either "puffeth up" and makes inaccessible, or else it humbles and invites confidence. Not all learning leads to wisdom, and not all experience adds to a man's humanity. And yet humanity is what it is expected to promote. As we grow older we suffer, we go on making the same mistakes, we acquire more and more material to work upon, we see deeper into motives, we pile up generalisations and panaceas, we evolve our own methods —always based upon previous experience—of sizing up people and situations and atmosphere and temptation and heaven knows what else, but if all this doesn't add up to a greater understanding it has lost its main purpose. "On disait que Poincaré savait tout et ne comprenait rien," says M. Maurois in his stimulating autobiography, "et que Briand ne savait rien et comprenait tout."

Whatever the way in which our experience comes to us, it is evidently a thing which we cannot do without. In the first place it is the most convincing of all arguments; in the second it is our only means of seeing life in proportion, in perspective. Even as children we instinctively feel this. Before we have reached the age of reason (itself a disillusioning term for a possibly disillusioning period), we are searching for experience. We are longing to have what is possessed by grown-ups, we are longing to *know*. It is only very much later that we realise what a bitter dead-sea fruit is the experience which comes of sheer human curiosity. Oh yes, it brings us knowledge all right, and it carries with it the obligation of making a good use of what we have learned, but it is far from being the best way of coming to our maturity. More safely, and incidentally more often, experience is forced upon us by circumstances and by suffering. This is the natural way, and nobody will deny that it is often bewildering.

Certainly neither books nor sermons, nor even the force of other people's lives, can do service for personal experience. What is it that gives the priest any sort of human confidence in the confessional? His knowledge of theology? Possibly, but much more the sense of having endured the same temptations. What, on his side, gives to the penitent that extra half inch of encouragement which makes him ready to take advice? The sinner need not want his priest to have been a sinner like himself, but he does want to know that the man who is helping him to get over his sin has fought with the same devils and been licked by the same flames. Indeed for no other reason was our Lord tempted like the rest of us: He "became sin" so that we might not feel that there were things which had never come His way.

It seems, then, that like a woman in labour, mankind is constrained to bring forth its finest contributions only as a result of struggle and sorrow and hardship and even, sometimes, of doubt and misgiving. What a tragedy it is, therefore, when so much good that has been arrived at after so much trouble is seen to be thrown away. Where experience is not drawn upon, or where it is drawn upon in the wrong way, there could hardly be human compassion. Where experience does not lead to love, it leads away from it. If we do not go out to meet other people's worries with a background memory of our own, we shall never be able to do them much good and may even do them harm. The rule of the text-book, the rubber stamp, the chalk line is only experience misapplied. Perhaps experience is one of God's greatest gifts to man—and because of this is capable of being put to such an extraordinarily bad use. God's gifts can be most exacting. St. Guthlac, pray for us.

HUMILITY AND RETICENCE

One Sunday when I was a small boy (one Sexagesima Sunday to be precise), St. Paul's account to the Corinthians of his hardships endured for Christ's cause came in for some slight critical comment from a ten-year-old contemporary of mine. Dom Leander Ramsay afterwards Abbot of Downside, had just read us the epistle of the day, and we of the Junior School were waiting for our milk and biscuits at eleven. My friend admitted to me that he thought it was rather "side" on St. Paul's part to mention so openly what he had had to put up with. "He does go on and on about it," was the complaint, "which, for a saint, seems to me a bit thick." For my part I was inclined to view St. Paul less strictly—excusing him on the grounds that after all he was a foreigner, and that perhaps in Corinth or Athens or wherever it was such boasting would not be considered odd. "All that sort of thing," I said, "is probably different abroad." But I could see that my friend was not convinced, and that he still felt St. Paul to have been too forthcoming.

Reticence is not always a sign of humility; it may be a form of pride. Far more often than a shrinking from praise, reticence is a shrinking from humiliation. Real humility doesn't mind, real humility takes risks. Becoming modesty and reserve are one thing, fear of making a fool of oneself is another. St. Paul in his letter to the Corinthians was not in the least afraid of being charged with boasting—in fact he charges himself with it—because what he really wanted to bring out was the fact that "the strength of Christ had enshrined itself in him". The process of thought in this long epistle is surely as follows: "I have put up with every conceivable kind of affliction for the sake of Christ. This might give me cause for self-congratulation, but as a fact it doesn't. Even if I had done all that I had been expected to do, I would still be an unprofitable servant. Much more likely to make me proud—or rather providing much more occasion for feeling gratified—were the supernatural favours which were heaped upon my soul by God. Now this *was* something. And I suppose I might have become proud—and so spoiled it all—if God hadn't at the same time taken away all sense of natural enjoyment about my peculiar privileges. The humiliation with which He has let me be flattened lower than the dust has blotted out both the pride of achievement and the pride of privilege. I would, at one time, have got out of this humiliation if I could. But I couldn't. I have had to make the best of it, fighting every inch of the way. At least now I can say this —that my humiliation has been in some way the greatest blessing of any that God has granted me. It has brought me so far down in my own opinion of myself that I have no self-confidence left. Before, with that list of heroics to my credit, I felt that there was much which I could do for God. Much, even, for which He might be grateful! With the knowledge also that extraordinary graces were evidence of His exceptional love for me, I might have gloried too much. I might have looked at myself and been pleased. But now! I can't trust in anything of my own. I therefore have to trust in Him." Surely this is what is meant by the conclusion which the Apostle arrives at: "When I am weakest, then am I strongest of all." It is worth while being not very reticent (even if it slightly shocks the British character) when at the end of it there is the admission of absolute personal insufficiency coupled with a confidence, which is as absolute, in God.

If we look into it, we find that St. Paul's experience is by no means unique. In a less defined way the same thing happens to most of us. If it isn't "a sting of the flesh to distress us" or "an angel of Satan sent to afflict us", it is simply the unfolding of life which does the work of wearing down our self-sufficiency. This is as it should be: we must let it. Not that we should jettison our enthusiasms—still less shrug our shoulders and say how hopeless we are at ever being able to get things done, and therefore why try to do them?—but that we should submit unprotestingly to the process whereby one by one our illusions about ourselves are peeled off. Only when we are what we are in the sight of God, do we fully enter into our full estate. And what are we? Nothing, absolutely nothing. Yet it takes us more than half a lifetime to recognise this. We have *got* to be humbled, we have *got* to face the fact that we are complete failures, morally and spiritually, before we are in any position to say with St. Paul: "When I am weakest, then am I strong."

Humility, then, isn't just backing away when there are more important people about. Nor is it saying things about ourselves which, however edifying it may be to say them, are depreciatory and untrue. Humility is truth. That is why St. Paul could recount without any false pride what he had done for Christ, and without any false shame what he was. Truth is not always nice to look at—especially when it is the truth about ourselves. Very often what the intellect is ready enough to accept in the abstract, the whole complete being, the *ego*, goes on resisting in the concrete. We may acknowledge our humble place in the scheme of things, while all the time our imagination, emotions, and memory are building pedestals on which we are only too willing to stand. So life *has* to be hard on us—in order to put us in our place. Painfully and by experience we have to learn how entirely unreliable we are. It is a truth which we are told from the start but which we never quite believe until the last of our self-sufficiencies have been exploded. Only then is humility capable of being perfected in our souls. There is just this to be added to what has been said—that if we are unwilling to learn the humiliating lessons of life and derive benefit from them, we lay ourselves open to discouragement, defeatism, and even possibly despair. Left without resources of our own, we either "cast all our care upon the Lord" and enjoy the promise of His support, or else we try our desperate best to find some sort of security in self-deception. This might be a solution if we could keep it up. But we never can. St. Paul's is the only answer.

OBEDIENCE AND LIBERTY

What we never seem to realise is that it is obedience, and not either rebellion or escape, that gives us our liberty. Fidelity to law is not slavery but emancipation. The opposite of established order is not disenthralment but disorder. Liberty does not mean enjoying the privilege of being able to break what laws we like; it means being able to live without inter-

ference within whatever system happens to be ours. The very
word "privilege", though the "lex" is restricted to "private"
application,[1] suggest that even the most favoured cannot get
away from law altogether. Nobody can pretend for long that
he is bound by no law, that he stands outside system, that he
can behave as if he were really independent. The most which
a so-called independent person can do is to elude one set of
laws and come automatically under another. Furthermore, by
a piece of poetic justice, the laws to which his new freedom
subjects him are nearly always far more enslaving than were
those which he shook off. Sooner or later the sinner must
recognise the fact that in this matter of getting his own way
and rejecting God's way, the best he can hope for is a process
of substitutions.

Take the obvious case of the man who decides to ignore
the laws of self-control and morality. In thinking to do away
with the moral law, he finds that the moral law will begin to
do away with him. He may derive great delight from defying the moral law, but he cannot bend it to his will. He cannot alter it. It will get him in the end. As Chesterton points
out about the law of gravity, if you try and break it from a
sufficiently high altitude, it breaks your neck. The moral law
works on the same principle: if you think you can break it
with impunity, it breaks you instead.

The Commandments of God are designed to make man
more free, not more frustrated. They are the rules which we
have to observe if we are to realise our function as men—let
alone as souls destined for the Beatific Vision. Disobedience
to these rules makes for a loss in our humanity, in our man-
hood, as well as our loss in grace. The man who refuses to
worship God, the impure man, the man who steals or kills or
is unfaithful to his marriage vows, is worse off *as a man:* he
has lost the moral and natural freedom to which he had a
right. The submission of man to the laws of God is like the
submission of matter to the laws of science. Science does not
impose restrictions upon matter; it liberates matter. Man is

[1] And so *privi-lege.*

freed by his obedience to God. The scientific parallel is worth developing.

It may be very irksome for a stone not to be able to swim or fly or speak or paint, but it would not be any more free if it could. It would be a freak. If a stone were to sing to you as you passed it in the road, you would know at once that it was a very bad stone. In the same way it may be very irksome for a man to remain chaste and sober, but if he does not he sacrifices his moral freedom. Just as the material law is the condition of material integrity, so the moral law is the condition of human integrity. The question of what would be more convenient does not enter in. The moral law is an absolute. Questions of great provocation, of insufficient knowledge, of muddled thinking, of following bad advice and so on, may explain the here-and-now violation of moral laws—and even to a certain extent excuse it—but they cannot for a moment condone it or say that under such particular circumstances the moral law did not bind. The inescapable fact is that we may not go against the order established for us by God—and that if we do we shall suffer for it.

Allowing that temptation is the desire to throw off the yoke of obedience, and get in a little sinning while the opportunity offers and while the mood is on us, we have to steel ourselves beforehand against what is the by-product of temptation— namely, the belief that the consequences of sin will not be as bad as the moralists make out. It is as well to remember that it is not the moralists who have made the law, and that it is not to the moralists that we shall be held responsible. Sin is to be gauged in terms of God.

"But when I sin," comes the plaintive protest to the above, "I don't think either of God or of the law. I think of myself." That is precisely the trouble: we always do. That is why, on the physical side, we have to know how to deal with passion and natural impulse and the mood to rebel; and, on the mental side, to keep the approaches clear both by refusing the occasions of sin and by repudiating the arguments in favour of indulgence.

"What about when the occasions of sin are all around one?"

is the next question which pierces the soul of the priest who has to listen to it. "What if everybody with whom one is associated assumes the state of sin as the normal? What if they don't think of sin, as sin, at all? What, again, of those sins which are not committed for the sake of sheer pleasure, but which for one reason or another one can't very well get out of? Surely there must be extenuating circumstances? For you to say that the approaches to sin can be blocked by such things as physical self-control and an intellectual grasp of principle is to make the thing sound more easy than it is. In practice there can be no such formula. For most of us in the world, we simply breathe sin . . . and on occasions it seems more honest, as well as more obvious, to do wrong than to do right." The bare mention of "extenuating circumstances" always (to me) sounds the alarm. But I suppose the problem must be faced.

In the first place even if every single member of the human race decided to go ahead and break the moral law, there would be no abrogation. The human race would still be bound by it. It does not mean that because every single member of the human race feels the urge to commit certain sins, *therefore* they are acting naturally in committing them. All it means is that since the fall of man, certain evil instincts are common to everyone. Impulses which, before original sin, were right, are now, though common to nature, wrong. They are wrong, not only because they are condemned by God; they are condemned because they are wrong for man. To claim exemption from God's commandments—or, which is far more usual of course, to excuse one's failure and inability to keep them— on the grounds of natural and universal instinct is to try and play off nature against itself. The instinct to oppose the natural law is in us only because fallen man is in revolt. The fact that everyone suffers from it is no excuse. We are all suffering from the after-effects of original sin. But we are also all given the means of countering this.

The second half of the objection has to do, not so much with the fact that "everyone does it so it must be natural, and therefore why shouldn't I?", but with the committing of sin either as an emergency measure or with a more or less good object in view. The plots of most novels and plays are variations on this theme. For example a son kills his mother in order to keep his family together, a wife commits adultery out of pity, a financier chooses the lesser of two evils and forges a signature. "Aren't there times," we ask, "when the moral law must give place to the general good? If to take life in war is permitted by God, surely a moral lapse or two which relieves another's loneliness and doesn't do any damage to a third party can't be very wrong? Once you allow that the law may be waived for one reason, I don't see why it shouldn't be waived for another—provided the reason is an upright one." By way of answer to this very common heresy, we might return to the parallel of material affairs being governed by material laws. Say you are unable to swim and that it is of absolute importance that you should get to the other side of a river before nightfall. You are blocked by material laws. It is no use your saying: "My reasons for reaching the opposite bank are legitimate and even lofty. Bridges and ferryboats are proof enough that the crossing of rivers without a knowledge of swimming is within the terms of the material law. But there happen to be no bridges or ferry-boats at hand. Therefore I feel justified in waiving one aspect of the material law in order to realise another. Kindly hold my coat while I confidently commit myself to the swirling waters." The moral law follows the same principle.

To conclude. There are many kinds of sinner, and there are many degrees of sin. Taken by and large, however, the division is between those souls who break the law and admit it, and those who interpret the law and excuse it. The degrees of sinfulness are, within these two divisions, infinite. With each degree of seriousness—that is to say, of malice—the supposed independence of the sinner is lessened. From the soul who weakly accepts the easiest way out, to the hardened blasphemer who fully means to hurt God, the relative harm done is to the person concerned and not to God. God cannot be harmed any more: we can be. There is no loss to the

Blessed Trinity when a man sets out to rebel against the order in which he finds himself: there is loss only to the man himself.

HOW THIS AFFECTS OTHERS

We have seen that to pursue an ostrich policy with regard to law is fatal. Denying the sandstorm by putting our heads in the sand can only mean, in the long run, more sand. Such a course is, as we shall try to show, anti-social as well. In other words we cannot, even if we justify our action on the plea that nobody suffers and that possibly some benefit, do harm to our own souls without damaging the souls of others. The law of charity is the most inescapable of all. The communion of saints is rivalled only by the communion of sinners.

It will be remembered that Mr. Honest in *The Pilgrim's Progress*, while recounting the opinions of Self-will, proposes the idea that a really upright man may allowably sin every now and then without doing much harm to anyone. The theory is that the vices of the virtuous are not really vicious at all. Insignificant weaknesses and no more. "Provided the upright man is genuinely against the sin in theory," is Mr. Honest's echoed argument, "it can't much matter his committing it in practice." To which Mr. Great-heart quite rightly replies: "A very wicked answer. For though to loose the bridle of lusts, while our opinions are against such things, is bad; yet to sin, and plead a toleration to do so, is worse. *The one stumbles beholders accidentally; the other pleads them into the snare.*" Passing over in all this the extraordinary likeness between Mr. Great-heart and Dr. Johnson, between Mr. Honest and Boswell, we see at once two things: first that if the upright man is genuine he will be the last to plead for a sympathetic toleration of his natural infirmity, and second that *any* "letting loose of the bridle of lusts" is a source of harm to others. It is this second point which concerns us here.

Whether another person is accidentally drawn into the oc-

casion of sin or whether he is "pleaded" into it, the truth is
that one man's sin is an evil which is shared. In some ways the
good man's sin has a worse effect than the bad man's: the
good man is looked to for a lead. It is not that the scandal is
caused, necessarily, by the suggestion of hypocrisy; more
often it is caused by the evidence of failure in one who was
believed to have been a success. There is nothing so disillusioning as weakness where there is expected strength. If people
knew the responsibility attaching to so-called strength of character, perhaps they would be less eager to acquire a reputation for it.

So close is the link between man and man that, apart even
from questions of scandal and indirect influence, there is no
such thing, strictly speaking, as a purely private or solitary
sin. All sin is public property. An apple growing on a tree
cannot say: "I have the peculiar quality of being able to go
bad without showing it. Now I find the strain of remaining
a sound apple too much for me. Therefore I will just go bad
inside, quite on my own, and none of the others need be in
the least affected." The apple cannot say this because it is
growing on a tree. It is part of the crop. Sooner or later, whatever it may look like on the outside, that apple will infect. A
human being does not belong to humanity in the way that
an isolated unit may belong to an institution of which there
happen to be any number of other units. He belongs to an
organism in which he is a "carrier" or "conductor". This membership is inalienable; he cannot get away; he may deny his
responsibility but he cannot shake it off. At times we all resent
some of the powers which have been given us by God: we
find them more trouble than we judge them to be worth, we
find them dangerous, we find them even—if we are not very
careful—working against ourselves. But we cannot pretend
that they do not exist. The power of being a moral factor in
other people's lives is one such power.

It is by the law of nature as well as by the law of grace
that we are morally linked together in this part-social, part-
physical, part-intellectual, part-spiritual order to which we
inevitably belong. The out-and-out sinner does not differ from

the ordinary Christian in his sin, but in his self-excommunication from the life of grace. The one is out of charity, the other is in it. The saint does not differ from the ordinary Christian in his sanctity, but in the completeness with which he allows himself to be assimilated in the circulation of grace. The saint is the perfect carrier. Sinfulness and virtue are relative; they are questions of degree; they do not divide mankind in the way that being in or out of charity divides mankind. For so long as the sinful soul is alive, he is roped up with the soul who is saintly. The moment a man kills his own soul by mortal sin, the rope is cut. He is alone. He suffers, and so does everybody else. A man may be out of charity, dead to grace, without anyone else knowing a thing about it. But throughout the whole organism there is a loss. Added to which, he will, sooner or later, actively infect the more immediate apples on the tree or in the basket. His so-called solitary sin rots him inside. His rottenness is bound to spread. We are all in it together.

THIS POWER FOR GOOD OR EVIL

Man may not be made for solitude, but neither is he made for multitude. Multitudes are too big, too impersonal, too imponderable (and, when you get down to it, too unlovable) for something so individual as the human being to feel at home with. Our first relationships are within a smallish circle, the family, and it is only later on that we begin to move in wider ones. From learning the lessons of charity at home, we go on to apply what we have learned to a society which numerically increases as we grow older. True, the Mystical Body comprises a multitude of members, but even the Body of Christ began as a baby.

For our charity to find its full expression—that is to say towards our neighbours as well as towards God—there has to be a neighbour as well as the will to be neighbourly. Our obligations, deriving from the service of God, are fulfilled in the service of individuals. When we have served the individual, we can think about serving the group, the community, the association of fellow countrymen, the human race and so on. The circle, for the saint particularly, can become very wide indeed. That is because of his greater charity.

It comes to this, then, that we benefit the Church by being of benefit to one another. The idea of helping the Church has a somewhat smothering effect; the idea of helping a person has not. When we think of the Church we think of the foreign missions, of crowds outside St. Peter's, of large-scale drives for this and that, of the Catholic Press, of the hierarchy and religious orders and subscription lists and bazaars. It is too much for us. We cannot help here. But we are forgetting that the Church means Christ. And that Christ means the individual member. And that *we* owe something to *him*.

Well, what do we owe to him? The answer is—whatever we have got and which he happens to be in need of. At least that is what the Gospel says. If our neighbour is in want, we have to go to the rescue. Our opportunities are infinite. The obligation covers a far wider range than the hundred and one varieties of ways in which material assistance may be rendered: it extends to the use of our talents, our sympathy, our readiness to forgive, and above all of our power to influence. It is absurd to say that we are not among those who are able to influence others. Everyone can. We all do—even unconsciously. If the responding spark is sometimes ignited without our knowing anything about it, what may not be done when there is the positive, active, apostolic will to be of use? Few lights are more often hidden under bushels—either thoughtlessly, lazily, irresponsibly, or for reasons of false humility—than this one of employing personal contact for the sanctifying of another's soul. You may say that it would be sheer hypocrisy on your part, and that you aren't any too sanctified yourself. You may say that such unwarrantable interference would be resented. You may say that you have other ways of serving God, thank you, and that He seems to be perfectly well satisfied by what you are giving Him. To all of which I answer that if a man genuinely wants to further both the cause of religion and the sanctification of his own soul, he must be ever on tiptoe to bring his personal interest to bear. He may have to exercise tact and self-control, he may have to do a lot more praying than he has done hitherto, he may have to make great acts of confidence in human nature—let alone in God's grace—and he may have to resign himself to the prospect of retiring into the background when the work is just becoming a source of gratification, but he may not evade the responsibility of giving out what he has got. He must scoop great spoonfuls from the depths of his experience, from the shadowed places of his own heart even, if by these means he may be able to satisfy another's hunger.

After all, how else can we help one another—save by giving something of ourselves? Signing cheques will not do it. Lending pious books—or writing them—will not do it. There is no substitute. (Why do people keep on writing books on the spiritual life? Surely twenty minutes spent in grappling with a particular person's individual difficulty are worth more than two hundred pages of generally administered written advice.)[1]

Now to turn to the other side of the subject, and see the harm which people can do to one another. In the foregoing chapter we dealt with the indirect spread of evil; what follows will be devoted to the influence of evil when it acts directly.

If, as we have seen, our responsibility towards others extends to those sins which we commit with no intention of involving anyone else besides ourselves, what must be the guilt of actively contributing to another person's destruction? Yet, given certain conditions with regard to the other person,

[1] On reflection the answer suggests itself that one is meant to do both—write for as long as one can find publishers who will take one's stuff, and grapple while the grappling's good. Nevertheless it is the particular which must be allowed to weigh more than the general. Thus if there were a choice, one's literary output should be sacrificed to one's correspondence and one's contacts. (Still more, if one is a priest, to one's confessional.)

we imagine ourselves exonerated from any sort of blame. So long as we have not been responsible for the other's seduction —and this does not only apply to matters of sex—we feel that we have only our own consciences to account for. To imagine, however, that provided the other person is corrupted already we have no further obligations is to miss one of the first implications of the Redemption. It assumes, incidentally, that the more corrupt such a partner is, the better our purpose is served. How can instructed Catholics forget that though the life of grace may have died in the soul, there is still the soul's immortality to be reckoned with? How can they forget that a soul goes on being a soul even though the chances of future happiness have been risked and lost? How can they forget that even if the existence of eternity is not realised, it is nevertheless in store for that soul—one way or the other?

"If they are prepared to go to hell," you hear it said, "that is their business, not mine. They probably don't believe in hell anyway. And if they do, they have qualified for it years ago. What sins *I* commit in that quarter won't make the smallest difference." In this question of a soul's eternal destiny, who are we to judge? Where heaven and hell are concerned it is surely presumptuous on the part of any man to rule out, on the grounds of profession or background or creed or previous record, the chances of another human soul. How can he possibly be sure? All he can know for certain is that his own relations with that other human soul will either prejudice or advance those chances. They will not have no effect at all. A man does not remain neutral as the result of coming in contact with another's vice—or virtue.

On one occasion when I was in hospital I was visited by a friend of mine who spent some of our limited time together telling me about his less creditable exploits in the army. Since this could hardly have been calculated to cheer me up, I can only suppose that the young man wanted to get it off his chest while I was judged to be in no condition to retaliate. However, I rallied sufficiently to deliver a spirited attack upon his criminal indifference to the claims of other people's souls. This aspect of his story had apparently never struck

him. About his own guilt he had been in no doubt; it was the
fact that other people's guilt might be laid to his door that
was news to him. Even when he had seen my point and was
duly shamefaced about his part in the whole thing, he con-
cluded his final review of the subject with the observation:
"Oh but that one was only an Arab girl, and so doesn't really
count." *Only* an Arab girl. Have Arab girls no souls? Are we,
then, *only* Christians? Ah, that's different. *We* may matter,
because we are meant for better things; *we* have been edu-
cated; *we* have at least got some sort of standards—even
though we don't keep to them. But as for people like natives,
harlots, perverts, crooks and genuine unbelievers, they needn't
cause us a thought: we don't have to worry about *their* souls.

But perhaps I am wrong about all this. Perhaps Christians
can behave as they do just because they can fall into a heresy
about themselves identical with that into which they fall
concerning those whom they look upon as outside the line.
Perhaps it is that they do regard themselves and their fellow
members of Christ's Mystical Body as *only* Christians, as insignificant parts of a concern which is too vast to have any
personal implications. But the Church does make personal
claims, Christ does invite a personal response, membership
is an individual thing. Hence the need to get back to the
idea which we suggested at the beginning, and awaken
within ourselves a sense of the closeness of our incorporation
in Christ. Unless we think of ourselves and other people as
younger sons in a family of those who have inherited the
promises of Christ, we shall be in danger of treating human
bodies, minds, and immortal souls as if they were so much
cattle. Our knowledge and experience of mankind, with its
complexities, with its hungers, with its insufficiencies, with
its supreme difficulty of adjusting itself to its divine and human relationships, must surely go far beyond the limbs and
brains of our fellow creatures. We are called upon by God,
and not merely by a few spiritual writers who happen to
have a particular point of view, to respect the place of each
living man, ourselves included, in the company of all those
who, however badly they may have followed the programme,

have, since the creation of Adam, been one with us in a common supernatural heritage. The family may be unwieldy and quite unimaginable. But that does not matter. It is still a family. It is a family which, for purely practical purposes, narrows down to those with whom, for good or ill, we come in contact.

THE POLICY OF TAKING

"I was brought up to believe that the main thing in life was work," wrote James Agate in the last of his books, "and that pleasure was in the nature of a treat. But there is a new spirit abroad. The only connection which the modern nose has with the grindstone is to snub it." The new spirit mentioned here, though not exactly unfamiliar in the pages of history, has certainly in the years following the war received new impetus. Perhaps it is a spirit which, shared by victors and vanquished alike, is in evidence after all wars. Perhaps having given so much and got nothing in return—for nothing has ever been got out of a war—there comes the opposite urge in man to grasp at everything and give nothing. High wages, short hours, pleasure, freedom from discipline, easier divorce and no obligations towards worship. It is sad to see money regarded as a substitute for labour and not as a reward for it. Sadder still to see marriage regarded as an escape or an excuse, to see pleasure taken to be an end in itself. Surely it is not an exaggeration to say that if a man gets his work and his marriage right, the chances are that he will get his soul right as well.

Take first the question of work. When a person's income or position is assumed to confer the right of making no further effort, it can only mean that leisure has been bought too dearly. In telling us that we must bear one another's burdens and so fulfil the law of Christ, St. Paul is outlining not only the principle of charity but the principle of labour as well. Indeed they are one principle: serving instead of grasping.

If, on the showing of the passage quoted above, the idea of being a servant to one's public is an ideal worth working for, it is all the more worth while to aim at being a servant to one's God. In effect there need be no conflict between the two. A worker serves God in mankind and mankind in God. Provided he keeps in mind the primary ideal of service, provided the motive is not self-interest first and last, his labour can never be entirely wasted. It may fail objectively, it may disappoint everybody including the worker himself, but so far as value in the sight of God goes it is a success.

In marriage no less than in work the whole thing turns on whether sacrifice of self or satisfaction of self is uppermost. Once the sense of mutual service is lost, the union is menaced by the source of all corruption—self-love. Unless marriage is undertaken as a vocation, with all the implications of mission and dedication, there is bound to be more grabbing than giving. Marriage has not been instituted so as to save people the trouble of living on their own—any more than religious orders exist for the convenience of their members. Neither marriage nor monasticism is intended to support people whose purpose is to lean. The real dividing line as regards mankind in general is not between the good and the bad—because the good can be bad and the bad can be good—but between the leaners and the non-leaners. The division is not even between the lazy and the energetic—because everyone is by nature lazy, and also because energy may be a purely physical quality—but between those who propose to contribute to life and those who expect life to wait on them. The question is a moral one, and not a physical or temperamental one.

Examine this in the light of the two most powerful emotions possessed by man, love and sorrow. If a man brings nothing to these emotions, if he either sits down and lets them take him in their sweep or else evades their responsibility and tries to escape them altogether, he is merely existing and not living. Passivity, after a certain stage, is not merely wasteful; it is morally wrong. To pursue a course of neutrality constitutes, eventually, hostility. A man becomes the enemy of

God's order. He reaps where others labour. Not only is it wrong, but in the long run it is folly as well: the individual is the worse off for not giving. The penalty of being a leaner is having your hand pierced by what you lean on. Your love turns sour on you, and your sorrow becomes insupportable. Only God can explain love and sorrow . . . and even then it calls for all the faith you have got if you are to accept the explanation.

Admittedly natural temperament plays a part in all this. But not as much as people make out. The essential part is played by the will. It is the will which in the last analysis must decide whether to take life in hand or let it slide.

AFFECTION, PASSION, AND SUFFERING

We have just seen that love and sorrow are two qualities which, escaping measurement and to a certain extent defying precedent, are the most likely among the emotions to jump the controls and stampede the spirit. The one can blow your judgement sky high, the other can pull your hope down to the dust. As in the previous chapter, so here: there are distinctions to be allowed for—which vary according to the individual temperament.

We know that love is not all heavenly; nor is it all earthly; it is a mixture of the two. What we forget is that some people are affectionate rather than passionate, others passionate rather than affectionate. There is hardly ever, in anyone, the right proportion of the two. That is why the question of love needs, in every separate individual, such careful handling. The balance, by adjusting the weights, by calling for acts of faith, of self-control, of even heroism, has to be maintained. Some among the more passionate natures are so lacking in affection that for longish stretches at a time they have no real love for anyone. This may not be their fault altogether; it may simply mean that what little power they have of affection is simply not operating. It is certainly their loss, and it must make the law of charity very irksome, but such people would be to blame only if they suppressed their affections and gave all their attention to their appetites. There is indeed the temptation to kill the gentler side of love—so as to feel more free in pursuing the side which is more gross.

Those, on the other hand, who are all affection and very little passion have their own problems. For them the attack on charity is less obvious. Their particular duty is to be tolerant of the failures which they see all round them, and for which they cannot find it in their hearts to feel any real sympathy. Taking their own experience as their index of reference, they are tempted to be either too hard upon the weaknesses of others or too easily shattered by the effects of these weaknesses upon themselves.

Where a passionate person makes perhaps too many allowances for other people's passion, an affectionate person not only makes too few but is over-conscious of, over-sensitive to the agony occasioned by someone else's blind desire. The trouble comes, of course, when somebody belonging to one category is married to somebody belonging to the other, and when there is a complete misunderstanding of each other's love. The passionate partner of such a union is puzzled and exasperated by what seems indefatigable sentiment, while the affectionate partner is hurt and disillusioned by what appears to be undisguised sex. It means that they have both limited the interpretation of love to their own experience, to their own emotion. Unless the first one recognises a devotion which is expressed by tenderness rather than by desire, and unless the second credits the other for not living entirely for sex, there is almost sure to be a breakdown of mutual confidence. The habit of love may be present in both of them, but if the form it takes is so different as to be intermittently violent in one and habitually demonstrative in the other, there has to be a more than ordinary understanding on each side for the preservation of any real harmony.

The point to be remembered during all this is that though the affections may be sickly and sentimental, may cling and exasperate, they do not damn. No soul has ever gone to hell for being too genuinely affectionate. The same cannot be said where the passions are concerned. On the other hand there have been many who have been saved by their affections. Nobody has ever been saved by his passion. If in this matter of love it is possible to canalise one's natural tendencies at all, surely people's natures should be steered away from the passionate element and towards the affectionate.

Love is too often regarded as a thing in itself—right or wrong—instead of as a fusion of two quite different things. By confusing desire and devotion we may be missing the means of securing a happy marriage. It is devotion after all, and not either excitement at one end of the thermometer or cloying sentiment at the other, which is the stuff of married life. Devotion is far more likely to be arrived at through the affections than through the appetite.

Consider now the other factor in life to which we have referred, and see how sorrow may, by being uncontrolled, waste a life every bit as effectively as the emotion dealt with above. As in the case of love gone wrong, misdirected sorrow may prejudice the happiness of others. We have seen on another page that it is not merely in bad taste but actually *wrong* to inflict our miseries upon other people; here we are thinking not so much about being a bore with our individual glooms as about being a drag with our habit of dependence and our demands. Dr. Johnson says that all noticeable unhappiness is a form of laziness. Laziness on the part of one involves extra pressure on the part of others. Sorrow indulged in, then, is anti-social, anti-charitable. We are not expected to deny, by a process of self-hypnotism, the existence of suffering in our lives, but we are, by a process of self-immolation, expected to keep quiet about it. If the humble man is the one who does not decry himself so much as forget himself, so the soul who is suffering properly is the one who does not repudiate so much as forget his claim to sympathy. The thing for him to do is to face his misfortune, accept it, and then suppress any further reference to it. This will not anæsthetise it, but it will at least insulate it.

Wise men sometimes say exceedingly silly things. Provided

a phrase comes out pat in the correct epigrammatic form, and can be seen to cover certain cases, nobody stops to think. "Nous ne sommes jamais aussi malheureux que nous le pensons," writes Romain Rolland, "mais non plus aussi heureux que nous le pensons." On this showing, a man may say to you, "You may not *feel* happy, but in actual fact you are—very", or "Without knowing it, you are a most unhappy person—in spite of that sense of general wellbeing which tells you that everything in the world is wonderful." Say you drink some rum after a cold walk. "Ah," you exclaim, "that has warmed me up." "Not at all," someone explains, "you are not as warm as you think. Rum has a certain effect upon your inside which creates an illusion of warmth. All it does is to make you *feel* warm." Exactly. Thank you.

Feeling unhappy may have any number of explanations, but none of them can explain it away. What is sometimes worse is that the feeling of unhappiness may have no explanation at all, no grounds for it whatever. But this does not dispose of it. The most a soul can do, very often, is to prevent it from spreading to others. A tortured spirit may have to go on being a tortured spirit until its release from the body of this flesh. The test of a soul is not how many sufferings it can be made to endure, but how ready it is to endure them—and keep quiet.

"But you are dealing with two quite different subjects under the one heading," is perhaps the objection. "Why not keep the problem of pain for a separate treatment?" Forgive me, but the fusion was intentional.

THE WIDE INWARD SPACES

What is it that can separate people who are obviously intended by nature and grace to be lifelong friends? Often we see people divided from each other as if by a wedge: people whose common interests and mutual affection should have the effect of uniting: people whom we had thought to be almost affinities. "The only great distances life contains are those we carry within ourselves—the distances which separate husbands and wives for instance. And so it will be with us." This, in the words of Paula to her husband Aubrey in *The Second Mrs. Tanqueray,* is the statement of the case. The speech which follows in the play provides an answer. "And then one day—perhaps very suddenly, under a queer fantastic light at night or in the glare of the morning—that horrid irresistible truth which physical repulsion forces on men and women will come to you, and you'll sicken of me." This provides, as suggested, *an* answer. But not the complete answer.

People do not sicken of each other merely because such an external thing as time comes along and parts them. Time can do no more than widen a gap which is already there. The point to get at is the reason for the gap. If the relationship has begun with a reservation on either side, a misunderstanding which has never been cleared up or a secret deliberately screened, then there is present all the material for what has been called above the physical repulsion forced by irresistible fact. There are no spaces so limitless as those of non-comprehension, and the tragedy is that these can exist where once there was understanding.

The description of Mistress Bubble in *The Pilgrim's Progress* shows us where such tragedies find their origin. "It was she that set Absalom against his father, and Jeroboam against his master. It was she that persuaded Judas to sell his Lord, and Demas to forsake the godly pilgrim's life. She makes variance betwixt parents and children, between neighbour and neighbour, betwixt a man and his wife, betwixt a man and himself, between the flesh and the heart." She told Mr. Standfast that if he would be ruled by her, she would make him great and happy. "I am the mistress of the world, and men are made happy by me" was her claim. The trouble is that so many listen and are taken in that, though none can find the happiness which is promised, she does in fact come to represent the world and dictate its spirit. She is the goddess of materialism, the enemy of faith and truth. Where her doctrine prevails there is hypocrisy, selfishness, and ultimately estrangement from the fellowship of man. In the Mystical Body of Christ there can be no such wanton distances as those which separate two souls who have walled off their understanding. It is only when the spirit of the world has been allowed to take possession, when charity has become petrified and greed has been allowed the control of policy, that a man is divided against his fellow men, against his family, against himself and his own best interests.

Perhaps as wide as the gulf which is caused by charity turned inside out is the gulf which a man feels in his own soul between what he could have been and what he is. He sees, thrown up with sometimes stark and irrefutable clarity against the screen of his soul, the ideal which once acted as the dominant force in his life and, alongside, the travesty which he has allowed it to become. The reproach is almost more than he can bear. He knows that to have failed after having accepted the summons is worse than to have gone back to the time before the offer was made: it were better not to have heard at all than to have heard and answered and not fulfilled. Here is a wide inward space indeed. The soul hopes against hope that God on His side will lessen the distance from His side, and allow no further wanderings away. If only the original purpose could be kept in mind, if only new desires could be fended off, if only the world would relax its grip and give a weak but well intentioned soul some peace . . . if only the soul did not admit of such deserved hunger, such agonies of hollowness, such emptiness and loneliness and guilt. The greatest distances are certainly those which we carry within ourselves.

SPIRITUAL WRITERS' CRAMP

One of the things which hinder a writer on spiritual subjects is the fact that he cannot get away from himself. His casebook is his own soul, his stock-pot is his own past, he is his own yard-stick.[1] It is a drawback to him for two reasons: first he is forced in upon himself, examining, weighing up, racking his memory, testing his good-faith the whole time— and this is bad, because the spiritual life is meant to be as objective as possible; second, his wares are thrown out into the open market—to be viewed by the curious and the critical as well as by those whom he is doing his best to benefit. He becomes like a poulterer who decides that the best way of satisfying his customers is to lay himself on the marble slab along with the pheasants and partridges. He is, in a true sense, "game". The customers, quite rightly, take advantage of this. Peering and prodding, the reviewers make comparisons. Deductions follow swiftly. It is, for the person on the slab, all very intimate and shaming. But then the price of having a public is the giving away, to a certain extent, of what is private; it is a price which any writer should be willing to pay. If he is sincere, an author is the servant of other —people the vast majority of whom he is never likely to meet —and service is always a privilege for which one has to pay. All the same, it does rather cramp one's style—to know that one is virtually making a general confession at Hyde Park Corner.

What has been said here does not apply only to writers on the subject of spirituality: it applies to all writers, but particularly, in the secular sphere, to poets, novelists, and dramatists. In a lesser degree are historians and biographers involved, while clearly it has only the most accidental connection with political pamphleteers, economists, and students of sociology. Every craftsman however—all the more so if he is a creative artist as well—betrays his personality in his work. He must do so. It is to a large extent through his work that he

[1] Of course it works both ways, because if he is fool enough to shy away from his own experience on the grounds of personal failure (or on any other grounds if it comes to that), he will show himself up pretty soon as an impostor. People know instinctively when he is drawing upon other men's findings. So it is safer in the long run to stick to what he knows from the inside—from his inside.

expresses his own essential and individual self. A man *may* find means of fluent self-expression over a tankard in an inn or across a kitchen table when discussing household expenses with his wife, but if we are looking for the normal signs of a man's development, if we want to discover traces of the incommunicable ego, we must examine the kind of impress a man's character has left upon his work.

The question for the individual worker to decide is how much or how little of himself he need—or possibly *must*—reveal. In order to make his work a true and finished realisation of what was originally conceived, he may not divorce the maker from the made. He not only may not, but cannot. He will expose himself somewhere. Certainly the history of literature has shown that whether authors have or have not consciously approached the question of self-revelation in their work, the question has in fact—though variously and according to the different natures involved—been decided. Some have obviously made up their minds to give away no more of themselves than they could help; others have gone the whole length and allowed the world to see them as, accurately or inaccurately, they have seen themselves. Others again, and let us hope that there are more of these than of any other, did not seem to mind what came to light about their interiors provided the main purpose of truth (or of art, or of politics, or of morality, or of whatever cause it was that they were trying to further) was served. Thus you get Dickens, for example, guarding the secrets of his own personal struggle, and putting people off the scent right and left. Not even Dickens could altogether cover up the frustrations which were his by circumstance and temperament. In another column you get such widely different writers as Tolstoi, Chesterton, Graham Greene, Dostoievski, Ibsen, Elizabeth Bowen, Mauriac, Virginia Woolf, Compton Mackenzie, Emlyn Williams, each in his or her contrasting way ready to reveal as much as anyone wants to know. Their essential natures, though not necessarily their moral conflicts or unique spiritual aspirations, are open to the skies. Finally you get a smaller group of writers who quite deliberately investigate the nature of man by carefully studying their own. These are they who tell the time by the ticking of their own hearts. Other people's problems, whether fictional or actual, are seen as projections of their own. Given right principles such writers, on account of their first-hand approach and intuitive grasp, can be enormously helpful in the world. All too often, however, they go round and round in circles—always coming back to themselves as the focus of interest. It is all right to start off from self, but it is a mistake to be so absorbed in the starting point as to be for ever returning to it. D. H. Lawrence, Stendhal, Proust, Flaubert, Joyce, Matthew Arnold are names which suggest themselves, but such a selection is entirely arbitrary and probably most unfair. At first sight it is curious that among this last company, whether or not you happen to agree about the actual names cited in the secular list, must be numbered most of the more widely read spiritual writers. This is not so curious when you consider two things: first, as already noted, that the field of research is necessarily the soul of the person writing; and second that, in the effort to suppress what is wrong about his own *geist* or *daemon,* the spiritual writer is letting off steam. This last point is worth a final paragraph.

It must be remembered that the writing of books is often for this kind of author the only outlet. Where another may find parallel or complementary forms of self-expression in rearing a family, in travel, in running a farm or an estate, in going to race meetings and the theatre, the ordinary writer of spiritual books must—particularly if he has not the active care of souls and does not play the piano or paint—work the creative urge out of his system somehow. The apostolic urge is only an aspect of the creative urge, and both find fulfilment of some sort in writing books about the spiritual life. If all this energy came forth in the form of fiction it would probably be an even greater release, as it was for instance in the case of Mgr. Benson, but it is probably true to say that when celibate writers take to telling stories out of their heads they tend to do so with more reference to their hearts than to their minds. Psychologists would tell us that where there has been no experience of passionate romance a good enough substitute may be found in writing about it. Rather than turn themselves into romantic novelists, authors with any sort of interest in the spiritual life are inclined, wisely, to walk on safer ground.

To conclude. Whatever we may feel about releasing the incommunicable ego, and allowing for the drawbacks already mentioned in this essay, it does seem to be worth while for a man to exploit any inclination which he may have towards writing for the benefit of his fellow men.[2] It will mean that he has not only to test his subject by his knowledge of himself, but that he has also to test himself by the practice of his subject. And this is very good for him indeed. The same is the case with regard to preaching: the value of what is said is measured by the sincerity of its source, and the source is valued according to the sincerity of its purpose. There are dangers of course: the writer may become an exhibitionist, he may be more concerned with his powers of perception and exposition than with what he perceives and exposes, he may cheapen his vision or use it for ambitious and material ends. There is no knowing what a man may not do with the gifts God gives him. But assuming that the soul has a right intention and is not deliberately unfaithful to its call, the dangers will be to him drawbacks only—and to be bracketed with the trivial little things which we considered at the start. It is always the same in the spiritual life: such dangers have power to cramp but not to crush. Does it so very much matter if our style is toned down and our freedom of expression is limited? So long as we set out to declare what we conceive to be God's word, and stand by that intention till the opportunity of doing so is removed, there is no great likelihood of spoiling the work either by exposing ourselves too readily or congratulating ourselves too soon. We have our critics to thank for this.

[2] The reflections expressed here are intended to counter the misgivings suggested on p. 41.

THE WEDDING WILL TAKE PLACE

"Has the moment arrived," young men will ask of one, "for me to propose?" "Do I," comes the question from the other side, "really love him?" As if we outside the thing could know! I have, in point of fact, suggested various lines to go on with regard to this subject,[1] but since the same sort of questions are still being put to me I can only suppose that I have not done it very well. It might be worth while therefore, avoiding repetition, to add a few afterthoughts here. (It is presumed that this book is being read by people living in the world rather than by monks and nuns. Though even a monk or nun could do worse than get up this subject. Indeed perhaps one reason why the present generation has seen so many unhappy marriages is because the teaching orders have had so little to say about what the sacrament of matrimony involves.)

To begin with, it is no good getting married on the strength of an idea. You are uniting yourself with a person and not a proposition. "It is time I settled down. Marriage is an enviable state. I must find a nice wife." And on the girl's side: "If I don't throw myself at some man's head, I may miss my chance altogether." The man has got to realise (or so I think) that it is better to be a bachelor all one's life than to marry the wrong girl; the girl must risk waiting—rather than take on someone she does not love. Admittedly people may get married from motives of loyalty, pity, protectiveness and so on, but even here it is difficult to see how the quality of love can be adequately replaced. You are not marrying a virtue, you are marrying another human being.

If, as we have just seen, it is hopeless to undertake marriage for a reason which is abstract, it is a no less mistaken approach to undertake marriage for a motive which is secondary. For example a man may choose a wife because he feels she will

[1] In *We Die Standing Up*. The relevant chapter is called "An Engagement is Announced. . . ."

run his house for him. If so he is marrying a housekeeper, and not a person. A man is meant to marry a partner to himself. He does not marry—even—a good mother to his future children; he is marrying, primarily, a wife. That she should be able to take her place at his side in society, that she should be possessed of the ordinary maternal instincts, that she is likely to be someone whom he can depend upon for companionship, for sympathy, for advice and so forth are obviously considerations which cannot be lost sight of. But first and foremost it is because a man loves a woman that he marries her, and not because he is either proud of her or in need of her support.

Very often love reveals itself in the discovery, within oneself, of some such need as we have mentioned—a need which a particular person is capable of supplying—but the need itself is not love. If a man embarks upon matrimony *simply* because he likes having someone to lean on, he will be disappointed. He had much better engage a secretary whom he will be able to get rid of if she does not suit him. Before leaving this aspect of the question we may note that the woman's attitude is to be judged somewhat differently from that of the man's. Since the care of the children, at all events in the early years, will largely rest with her, it is more her responsibility to see herself as a potential mother than it is his to see himself as a father. Most of what has to do with the home will be her province: she must therefore assure herself that she loves the man sufficiently to make that home an agreeable place to live in. Though a man may not marry because he wants to lean, a woman should be quite clear, before she marries, that she wants to be leant on. Unless she wants this, she is not in love.

The natures of man and woman are, with all their dissimilarities, sufficiently alike in this—that for the fruition of any sort of real love between them there has to be on each side a sense of spiritual, intellectual, emotional, and physical correspondence. The harmony can never be absolute, but touching all four points there should be at least the agreement of essential sympathy. One might narrow the thing down and say that the human heart operates on two valves, both of which have to be functioning in the man and the woman alike. Not necessarily in him and her *equally*, but in him and her together. Not necessarily to be expressed *in the same way*, but in him and her at the same time. Call one valve affection and the other desire. Often there is love on his or her side but not in the full sense, not coming from both valves. For loyalty and devotion and all the lasting qualities which go to make up the lifetime, love's first valve is drawn upon; marriage's other requirements are supplied by the second. The whole heart has to be given—in exchange for another's heart, equally whole. Not for the sake of what comes of the exchange is this given, but for the sake of giving.

THE SUITABLE MATCH

A marriage which is only a suitable one and no more is not likely to suit either husband, wife or children indefinitely. "But," protests someone who is on the verge of getting engaged, "this would mean that half the marriages in the world ought never to have taken place. Am I not supposed to select my partner in life because of what we have in common —background, interests, friends, upbringing and so on?" To which I would answer unhesitatingly that though it would be absurd to discount these natural and social bonds, it would be very unwise indeed to let them bind you for life if there is doubt about the more important element of love. There is an affinity which has nothing to do with what is shared outwardly, and this is the affinity which, for marriage, matters most. Suitability is the staunchest support to love, but it is not a substitute for it. A suitable match without love is more of a risk than a love match without suitability.

"If you rule out loveless but socially correct marriages," it might be argued, "your next step will be to rule out marriages which, though possibly in the strict sense loveless, are undertaken out of admiration." The answer to this one must depend upon what construction is put upon the word "admiration". The trouble is that it is so hard to know what people mean when they say that they "admire" someone, that they "are devoted to" someone, and so on. If it is a question of mere mutual respect and nothing warmer than that, then (in my opinion) there is not enough to go on for purposes of marriage; there is not enough here, even if it is backed up with a sense of reliance, to warrant the hope either that the real thing will somehow emerge out of it all or that the general goodwill felt on both sides will supply for the love which is lacking. If, on the other hand, admiration is taken to mean the sort of heroine-hero-worship which has in it more than immature sentiment, if it is understood to be that kind of appreciation of each other's natures which makes for a sense of feeling at home with one another and a desire to be always together, if it stands for the kind of reverence which does not in the least chill but which induces a conviction of one's own unworthiness, if it is the admiration which inspires confidence where perhaps there was none before, then, even though the "grande passion" may be absent, there is here surely the makings of love. Enough of it, anyway, to get married on. Not everyone, after all, is built for this "grande passion" business. Many people have never known, and never will know, the sense, humiliating and ecstatic at the same time, of being at the mercy of an emotion which is so overwhelming that it could make them throw over everything that they had been brought up to, worked for, lived with, and send them off to the end of the world at the lifting of an eyelid. Certainly it would be the last purpose of this essay to debar such souls as these from the chances of happy married life. Perhaps most marriages are made and kept together by those who have never experienced the particular invasion of their stability just mentioned. I really do not know. All I know is that there can be love where there have been no such crises. The course of love is proverbially uneven, and often there may be outbreaks of violent desire and even of what appears to be violent hate, but love is essentially a habit and not a series of upheavals. The initiation may have an upheaving effect, and its several expressions are undoubtedly more dynamic than static, but, residing as it does chiefly in the intellect and will —then only in the emotions and the senses—its activity is constant rather than intermittent and explosive. Unique, if you like, in its experience, but ordered in its possession.

To return to the subject of these paragraphs, we notice that the term "suitable" may indeed be stretched to cover more than what is merely appropriate and fitting. Given the union of affection, the more "suitable" the union is in other ways the better. All that is claimed here is that love alone can effect the identity of purpose which is needed to keep two people happily together. If similarity of outlook were enough, then those who made pleasure their chief concern would be found to make the best husbands and wives. The purpose which is fashioned into one thing by two souls who are in love with one another is something very different from the common interest which is so often mistaken for it.

"But even after all that", complains our heckler at the last, "I don't see why, lacking the authentic impulse and the sense of unworthiness and the urge towards self-dedication and the rest of it, one shouldn't quietly marry someone nice. Just because she's nice." One may. But one has to have a pretty strong longing for her niceness—together with an equally strong longing to be worthy of it by being nice oneself. Which brings one back again to being in love. It is not only the niceness that one is wanting: it is the girl herself: and this is right. Go forward, young man . . . God's blessing is upon you.

All this looks very complicated on paper, and it may seem an almost insoluble tangle when the mind is trying to decide whether the essentials for marriage are there or not. But if the soul is set towards God and not towards selfish satisfaction there ought to be no real danger of making a mistake. In the nature of the case the issue is nearly always bound to be confused. Our terms of reference are unreliable, our judgement is disturbed by the romantic atmosphere created by the emotions, our friends are too far outside us to be able to give us the advice we need. The great thing is not to let one sphere of activity dominate the rest: physical, emotional, and spiritual claims must be looked at in their respective contexts. For most people the temptation is to allow the body to do service for, and ultimately override, the heart and soul. This is because the mind is always in danger of being pulled down to the level of the flesh: the mind is able to appreciate and take part in physical enjoyment, while the flesh is incapable of appreciating or taking part in the satisfactions of the mind. The demands of the body for its own kind of satisfaction are, therefore, all the more insistent. For most people the greater pull comes from the body, not from the mind. But, as we have seen in this essay, there is always the possibility that reason—giving as grounds the "suitability" of embarking upon this marriage rather than that—may quash all other claimants. History and individual experience have shown that reason can be a tyrant. If in the private sphere, reason, unaided by grace or natural inclination, takes it upon itself to choose an appropriate mate for a man, and if body and heart and soul are ready to fall in with the idea, the outcome can hardly be a triumph for reason—since the unsuitability of the match will show itself eventually—and will certainly be a tax upon body, heart, and soul such as it is not in the nature of marriage ordinarily to impose.

CORRESPONDENCE COURSE

"Friendships, love affairs, infatuations—they are all hell." I quote, with permission, from a letter. The writer is an artist. Artists may tend to be extravagant in the expressions of their ideas, but they do at least express them. It is often when they have expressed them with some force that other people, not artists at all, discover that the ideas are theirs as well. It is because I believe the feelings expressed in this letter to be fairly general that I record them here. My own part in the business will be merely to state the case against.

"You write and say that you would like me to meet your friends, and that it would do me good," my correspondent goes on; "but I don't even want to meet my own. If mine don't do me any good, yours aren't likely to. Thanks all the same. Pictures and books for me in future: they don't hurt so much. With regard to people, the only solution is the traditional one which worked so well in the old Ottoman Empire: get hold of the girl and put her under lock and key. At least you know then where she is and what she's up to. Whereas if you take this young woman I'm after, how she . . ."[1] But, my dear artist, don't you see that the moment you start locking up your loved ones and labelling them as your own, you are putting ideas of independence into their heads? You can gaze at this young woman of yours all day, and the chances are that she will love it, but if you once put her under a glass and gaze at her as if she were your own private exhibit, she will turn her back, break the glass, and walk off. What's more, I don't altogether blame her. It's no good your growling "how she's got the nerve" into your beastly red beard, and cracking a couple of mahogany palettes across your knee. It's as natural for her not to want to be monopolised by you as it is for you to want to monopolise her. This oriental instinct of yours to possess absolutely is not confined to you and the Ottoman Empire; but then neither is the instinct to escape absolutely confined to your young woman and Chelsea, S.W.

Friendships, love affairs, infatuations may indeed be hell; but who ever said they would be heaven? For years we have been led by script-writers, poster-painters, romanticists and crooners to expect unmixed bliss from the exercise of our affections. There is nothing, however, in the charter of human nature to suggest that the most vital of all human emotions should be exercised without cost. Love is not a luxury, and those who have learned anything about it understand this well enough: they would not have it otherwise. If you are talking about the sudden flirtation of an hour, or the uprush of sentiment which you may feel towards a total stranger, then quite possibly the sweetness *is* unimpaired and gratis. But who wants sweetness anyway—when he can have reality?

[1] There is no necessity, whatever the reader's curiosity, to quote further.

You do not have to pay much for a fleeting taste but you do for truth. Besides, if love is not all heaven, it is not all hell either. Only by seeing how near love can be to hell does a soul come to realise how near it can be to heaven.

Books and pictures will never do instead of people. In our more disillusioned moments we think that perhaps they may, but when we have recovered from the emptiness of being let down we know that they cannot. This need not be elaborated, illustrated, or even defended. The books and paintings themselves convince us of their insufficiency. Be honest, my good artist, and see if you would exchange that young woman of yours, in spite of her mercurial intransigence, for the Bodleian or the National Gallery.

I REMAIN, INDIRECTLY YOURS

Lady Oxford used to say that one could never really influence weak people but only strong ones. Thus if in the last analysis it is the receptivity of the subject which makes another's influence operative, then the benefit must necessarily depend upon how long this readiness to respond is to last. If the mood is a passing one and there is again a readiness to respond to a new ideal or impulse or challenge, then the character is said to be weak; if on the other hand there is a reiterated acceptance of whatever it was that had the stirring effect, then the character is strong. It all depends upon whether what is received is assimilated, becoming part of the permanent structure of the person's make-up, or whether it is just played with. All this is perfectly obvious. The only difficulty is that the question is begging itself. What is there to prevent a so-called weak person assimilating a permanent habit of acting weakly? What is there to prevent a so-called strong person obstinately following a course which is at variance with his strength? When you get down to it, you are faced—so it seems—with only an artificial distinction between the weak and the strong. There is the uneasy feeling that we are all in the same boat, that we are all weak. I don't know what Lady Oxford would have said to this. Probably in her decisive way she would have said, "Of course we are, my dear man, but there's no earthly reason why we need be."

Perhaps the answer is that though all may be born weak, all, as they grow to maturity, can, by choosing to be influenced by one lot of objectively stronger personalities rather than by another, become strong personalities themselves. This seems to cover it. As a formula it also allows for the action of grace. If you divide the world into the weak and the strong, you complicate rather than simplify the problem of free will. If, on the other hand, you assume (with me) that we are all pretty weak anyway and that it is a question of who is going to leave the deepest impress upon our malleable natures, you immediately leave the door wide open for both the soul's individual response to grace and for the action of grace operating through the instrumentality of a fellow human being.

People like to think of the weak as belonging to the blancmange or jelly-fish class. Most unhappy and inaccurate comparisons, both of them. Neither the blancmange nor the jelly-fish is capable of receiving an impress from without. Both, in fact, are magnificently resilient. You cannot dent a blancmange—as you can, for instance, dent the tin from which it plopped—nor can you sway the essential nature of the jelly-fish. Short of scooping out spoonfuls from the one and dismembering the other, you cannot be sure that your influence is having any effect at all. It is no good talking about "strength" and "weakness": the terms here do not apply. Similarly with regard to people's characters, the terms can but have a relative connotation. Much better employ words which mean something—such as "yielding", "resilient", "obdurate".

We have seen, then, that from the point of view of the person who is exercising the influence there is no guarantee that any direct effect will follow, and that from the point of view of the person influenced there is no knowing what, if anything, has been received. We are like a lot of people bumping up against each other in the dark. We may lash out and hit nobody, or we may turn round too suddenly and knock somebody over. There is no limit here to the scope of the action of grace.

This curious absence of recognisable link between cause and effect in the impact of character upon character is borne out very strongly when, for instance, we do our utmost in a particular direction for certain individuals and the result is something absolutely different from what we had planned. A good result of some sort may be achieved, but if so it is almost in spite of us rather than because of us. There seems to be no relation between the direction of our work and its final fruition. It is as if our effort, enthusiasm, weariness, anxiety, prayer, penance, and all those hundred things that go into the business of caring for individuals' souls have to be put through a process before they can bring about what has all along been in the mind of God. Broken into small pieces, ground to powder, mixed into a paste, and then recast in a new—and sometimes to us a not personally-gratifying—mould. But if the shape which emerges in the end is not always what we would have chosen, it is at least nearer to the pattern than anything which we had ourselves conceived. What it all means is that God has sown, we have labored, and God has come back again to bring in the harvest. His harvest, not ours.

If we were granted to see the consequences of our labour, if we were able to check up directly and say, "I gave him that side to his character which everyone finds so pleasing," we should be leaving God's action out of account altogether. If we are to glory at all (and it is not expedient indeed) we should glory in being chosen as instruments; we dare not take the credit for more than this. Our function may almost be said to cease when we have done our best and handed the outcome over to the disposition of Divine Providence. It is no good worrying any more after this. The good has been done, and the effects must be allowed to work themselves out secretly. The growth in holiness which we have prayed for may be finding expression on another plane, in a different dimension.

The best influences are usually those which are indirect:

they are better for both the person influencing and the person influenced. Otherwise the one becomes oppressive and the other oppressed. Plato knew this when he said that "you cannot make people good; the most you can do is to provide the conditions in which the good life may be lived." The effort to create those conditions is the surest guarantee that the good life will be lived. There is no absolute guarantee. The only absolute guarantee is that the effort will not be wasted: God will apply it somehow, somewhere, to someone. It would be nice for us, though not so sanctifying, if the people we sacrificed most for in this world were able to come to us with their recognition of our service. "I owe you everything," we might hear. And how very bad for us it would be. The existing system is far safer: there are no all-compensating satisfactions, no triumphs of achievement, no convictions about blood being well spilled and tears being profitably shed. If man's communication with God is by faith and for the most part indirect, it should not be so surprising that the most essential communication between man and man should be conducted upon the same lines.

UNEVEN RESPONSE

I have just been giving a very dull, but I suppose necessary, instruction to two young people who are engaged to be married. It is a routine obligation for all three of us, and I am not likely to meet either of them again when the course is finished. She is the Catholic and the one who is making all the running. In her can be seen, shining incandescent through the drabness of background and future prospects, the love of her religion, the love of her family, the love of her young man, the love of unborn children. In him can be seen practically nothing. Nothing that is to say, which gives promise of a happy married life. The wonder is that he has got as far as this, and why he thinks he has got a chance of making a success of it. It must be all her doing: the stronger personality, the one in whom love is a driving force, pushing the thing along. My instinct is to advise them strongly to call it off; if I get a chance I shall.

Now this is the point which I want to make here—that where love does not unite, it actually separates. The separation is all the more effectual for being, on one side, unrecognised. The undermining process of a love which is out of tune may go on for ages and not declare itself until, for the one who loves, it is too late. In the case which I am considering, it is strictly speaking the girl's love, rather than the man's lack of it, which is likely to menace the happiness of their marriage. It seems that where love is not received on its own terms, where its course is not allowed to run exactly true, the very quality which brings two people together is the one which holds them apart. Like the mortar between two bricks: from one point of view it unites them, from another it comes in between. Love can come in between.

A love, though it may be as spiritual and unselfish as you could wish to find on earth, may not only, by being out of tune with the emotions of the person loved, put up barriers which seem to grow in size and number as time goes on, but can elicit the sentiment which is its exact opposite. Hate and disgust can result from being either unwilling or unable to respond to the demand of love. That is why it is such a false heroic for the one who is loved but does not love, whatever the reasons of so-called honour, to keep silent and let the arrangement stand. It may begin with heroism, but it will end in hypocrisy. Oceans of misunderstanding must flow in where the shores of one personality are not properly recognised by the other. That there should be a fog in this particular channel is dangerous; that an attempt should be made to hide in this fog is disastrous.

There is this paradoxical quality about love, that it either sees intuitively or else is so unperceptive that no amount of evidence is any use. The reaction is either hair-trigger and immediate, or else non-existent. Insufficiencies which are patent to all the world are not admitted by the lover . . . while at the same time all sorts of far more subtle and secret movements of the mind which the outside world would miss completely are known instinctively. The human heart has its own way of knowing, but there are curious contradictions among the things which it knows. It is possible for love to be sensitive to everything except the truth.

To conclude. When a generous and ardent love has as its object someone either base or empty or lazily afraid there sometimes arises an estrangement which gives the ultimate revelation a bitterness which is all the more tragic because avoidable. Ultimate revelation there is bound to be, and then the revulsion is likely to be mutual. If the revulsion were merely one-sided, and on the side which deserved it, the harm done would not be so great. But more often than not the damage is greater to the soul who is disillusioned than to the soul who is responsible for the disillusion. Now is the time, after the fog has lifted, when the highest heroism is called for—on both sides. Marriages can, and do, survive this ordeal, but it is hardly fair to put them to the strain of it. How I am going to put all this across to my young couple at the next instruction I have not the faintest idea.

THE *OPPOSITE* SEXES

In the doubts and speculations which are inseparable from the emotion of love, the mistake which is made by both women and men alike, is to imagine that the other person's attitude can be judged by a careful investigation of what one happens to feel, or might be likely to feel, oneself. I have touched upon this subject before, so will not go over it all again. There are, however, some additional notes to be made, and further comparisons to be taken into account. In this business of "all for love", a man's interpretation is found in practice to be different from a woman's. They may both mean the same thing by it, but their natures make for a different expression of it.

A man or woman, then, may calculate from the findings

of self-examination till he or she is black in the face, but the fact must remain that the sources of reference are not the same and are therefore misleading. It is seldom that a man can know what is going on in another man's mind; hardly ever can he know what is going on in a woman's. With insight and experience in his favour, a man may have a pretty good guess as to what most men would feel under given conditions, and from this he may conclude how they might reasonably be expected to act, but unless a woman is a very shrewd woman indeed, and is possessed of a mentality more masculine than feminine, she can form only the most general idea.

In the matter of love, either sex is in a position much the same as that occupied by the human mind with regard to the animal mind. Obviously the contrast is not as sharp as this, but it is analogous. We human beings can follow the processes which go on in the lower degrees of creation but we can follow them only a certain way: our knowledge, though true as far as it goes, is so rudimentary, so incompletely parallel, that it is really no safe guide. For instance I know that a horse would rather look at a stack of oats than at a tram. I know also that most horses would be happier in a hunting field than in a stable. But it is straining my knowledge of horses too far if I attempt to estimate the individual horse's mental processes any closer. I cannot be sure with any degree of accuracy what horses as a whole—or even the particular horses with which I am acquainted—think of diet, hunting, and loose-boxes. Such knowledge is beyond my range. Similarly the way in which a woman loves is beyond my range—because I have never been a woman any more than I have been a horse.[1] I can observe certain effects

[1] Again it must be insisted that there is no question here of one sex being higher or lower than the other. The analogy might just as well have been taken from the angelic instead of the animal order. I do not, for example, know what an angel thinks of hunting, trams, and loose-boxes. The angel's thought can be followed only when it coincides certainly with our own, more limited, processes. On the subject of worship, for instance, we are at one.

and I can listen to what women tell me about their young men, but because I can never experience what a woman experiences I am virtually in the dark. My common human nature carries me some of the way, but my sex carries me no way at all. In fact it makes me look in the wrong direction. When analogous knowledge is pressed too far it turns inside out and becomes ignorance. When we say that people are too clever by half, it usually means that we think them not half as clever as they ought to be—or as we are.

The above is merely by way of introduction. What follows has to do not with generalisations which cannot be made, but with the few which can. One of these I make without hesitation—namely that a man's love is nothing like such an over-all emotion as a woman's. For instance a man is not in love every moment of the day; a woman is. This may be due to nature's way of allowing for the respective functions of husband and wife, of fatherhood and motherhood. The man has to go out to work, the woman has to take care of the children. Thus man's affections may be so planned in the order of nature that he *has* to forget, or he would fail as a husband and a father. In the same way perhaps the woman's capacity for affection is designed for the whole-time work of looking after the home. There is an elemental difference between the masculine devotion which provides for the family, and the feminine devotion which lives with it. This is why men are made more versatile, more quick-change, than women: their place in the natural-social-domestic scheme requires it.

Such divergence is seen for instance in the way in which a man's mind readily departmentalises, keeps its affections and its passions separate; the woman's mind views love much more as a whole. The woman takes on love in its completeness or not at all; and having taken it on, cannot lightly depart from it. Let me illustrate this. It is possible for a man living away from home to take a strange woman for the night, satisfy his passion, and then sit down next morning after breakfast to write a perfectly sincere and affectionate letter to his wife. It is incongruous, it is monstrous, it is morally indefensible, but it is possible. I have known it happen. Some men, believing themselves to be loving husbands, would think nothing of it. "Dearest Mary, I am only waiting for the day when I can get back. . ." Perfectly genuine. Now in the case of a woman such conduct, *mutatis mutandis,* would be impossible. Her mind would not work like that. She would feel either the shame or the absurdity of the situation so clearly that there would be no question of writing that sort of letter next morning. Even if she forced herself to making an expression of conjugal affection she would know she was striking a hopelessly false note. Not so, necessarily, the man.

It is not that men are naturally hypocrites and unfaithful, but that some men can be unfaithful without feeling hypocrites. And this few women can manage to do. Men are so made that they are able to go on loving their wives in circumstances where it would be impossible for their wives to go on loving *them.* What is a contradiction morally need not be a contradiction psychologically, and this is where women have the supreme advantage over men. The mind and heart of the woman operate on the one cylinder. The result is that the woman tends to be both more logical and more faithful than the man.

Much of what has been said here will, I am afraid, make disturbing reading for the wife. Much will, I hope, make shaming reading for the husband. The point is surely that if both wife and husband can be brought to recognise their own and each other's natural differences and tendencies, they will be at once more careful, more thoughtful, and more tolerant. Married love cools through want of sympathy and understanding—not through want of married love. The love can remain if it is given a chance. Time, and even failures on either side provided they are regretted and not excused, need not kill married love. Somerset Maugham, in his play *The Circle,* makes Lady Kitty say that the tragedy of love is not death or separation—people can put up with these—but indifference. The dramatist takes it for granted, as do a number of authors Catholic as well as non-Catholic, that the tragedy is inevitable and that love not only does not, but cannot, last. If you confuse the substance with the accidents, and do not take the trouble to safeguard either, of course it will not last. But there is no earthly reason, intrinsically, why it should not. The doctrine of inevitable indifference is the most poisonous doctrine, and I for one have every intention of attacking it. Perhaps the truth which is least stressed by Catholic writers is the truth that love can be made to last. With prayer, selfless devotion, obedience to Gospel principles, its permanence is guaranteed. "I am only waiting for the day when I can get back": this can ring true at any time, and without the aperceptiveness with which the phrase has been connected above.

HISTORY REPEATING ITSELF

"The future," says Paula in *The Second Mrs. Tanqueray,* "is only the past again, entered through another gate." Some people's experience would doubtless contradict this statement absolutely, but for the majority it must remain profoundly true. However varied our circumstances, however altered we feel ourselves to be under the rough handling of life, there is always a thread running through our story which makes before and after sound irrelevant. Past and present seem so much of a piece—with the present proving how unavoidable are the lessons to be learned and yet how unlikely it is that they will be—that we tend as we grow older to drift along in a state of practical, though theoretically repudiated, fatalism. Round and round again come the problems which we met with years ago and never fully solved. We wonder if we shall ever shake them off. Our attitude towards these problems tends to crystallise with each new experience of them: our attitude is largely determined by whether we are prepared to be saints or whether we are content to be cynics.

The truth expressed by Pinero in his play was not viewed by the speaker from the same angle as by the saints. Where Paula Tanqueray was thinking of inevitable repetition, the saints would pick up the same idea and see in it renewed opportunity. To one kind of soul the future is an inescapable return of the wheel, to another it is an extension of the free and unconditioned chances of the present.

"If that were the case," it might be objected, "only the fatalistic and cynical would experience the sense of repetition. These idealists of yours would merely drift along, hoping for the best and comparing nothing of their present experience with the past. Whereas it is surely something common to everyone, whether cynic or saint, to hear echoes ringing down the valleys of his life." Certainly there is the same continuity in both good and bad: all that is claimed here is that where a soul who is looking for God will recognise the continuity of grace, the soul who is looking for excuses will see nothing but the force of necessity. Continuity comes in right enough, because we cannot dispense with cause and effect. The mistake is to imagine that the effect is preordained and that we have no control over the cause. Thus to say that in the history of the world the same sorts of crises and movements recur is not to point to caprice or determinism; it is merely to point to the consistency of human nature: people go on acting, freely, in the same way. Similarly in the history of an individual: the cycle of happenings depends very largely on the twist given to it, freely, by the person himself.

Take the question of sin and temptation—always easier for purposes of illustration than the impulse to virtue. The reason why the same sort of temptation has to be faced again and again is not that such accidents as chance or heredity are playing merry hell with one's state of grace and conscience, but that with every concession to the existence of temptation a further breach is made in the defences against it. This is obvious, but what is not quite so obvious is that even if sin has never been accepted in the will, the fact that the soul has admitted the possibility as a practical consideration, has owned to an affinity with the sin, has come to see that sort of temptation as part of itself and its normal life, has settled down to live with it as a congenital tendency is more than enough to account for the repeated attacks along

that particular line. In allowing too much for the resumption
of the offensive, the soul lays itself open to unnecessary en-
gagements. Where one person will resist a temptation because it is simply not upon the agenda, another will consent
to the same temptation because it is the kind of thing he has
learned to expect.

Thus it is in the devil's interest to induce the attitude of
mind which says, "This business is clearly going to stay with
me all my life; I suppose I must simply put up with it." This
sounds like resignation to the dispensation of Providence, but
in actual fact it is perilously near to defeatism. It sounds like
waiting for the harvest when the cockle will be separated
from the wheat, but in actual fact it is telling the cockle to go
ahead and stifle the wheat. It is one thing to admit the existence of cockle and quite another to give it permission to
grow. To sit down hopelessly among the cockle stalk[1], while
gazing wistfully at the ears of corn, is to ask for trouble.

When temptation gets its hold on a soul, it is because that
soul has dallied somewhere. The person may not have wanted
to sin, indeed he may have wanted very much *not* to sin,
but he has wanted the fun of being tempted without the
pain of being guilty. Nobody plays with fire because he likes
being burned: he plays with fire because he likes just not being burned. A man may run away from sin for a variety of
reasons and in mixed dispositions, but unless he does so with
the determination of increasing the distance between himself and the temptation he will find that sin will catch him
up. Most of our failures are due to the sneaking hope that
temptation, though thrown off for the moment, is still running
after us.

What has this to do with the original proposition? It
means that when a soul, looking back upon its failures, con-
cludes that the past will enter again through another door
and that nothing more may be expected of the future, he
has as good as given in. Instead of looking at the past or the
future, he should be looking at the door. The door can be
opened or shut freely according to his will.

[1] If cockle has a stalk.

RESTLESSNESS

To say that the inability to settle down in any one place or in any one work points infallibly to weakness of will, to instability of character, is an over-simplification of what may be a complex psychological problem. "Exactly," you will say, "that's just what I meant: the man who is restless wherever he is must be a neurotic of sorts . . . and is therefore either weak in the will or weak in the head. Precisely what I intended to convey." But wait a minute. What about there being misfits in the world who are possibly meant to be misfits? Who could not be anything else? Who fit into the landscape precisely because they are the unexpected shape? Who, in the long run, positively add interest to the picture instead of taking away from it? Who are we, with our absurdly limited vision of the over-all scene, to say who fits and who does not? Seen close up, the supposed misfit may seem to spoil the composition, but if we walk back and look at the thing from a distance, more from the point of view of God who is responsible for the composition and the development of a likeness, we stand a better chance of appreciating the misfit's position. We have to make concessions if we are to discover what the artist is about, and perhaps the first concession is that of admitting that what looks like muddle, confusion, awkwardness to man may well appear harmonious to God.

The whole of creation proves that God prefers variety to uniformity: He could have made one shape of mountain, one shade of sky, one smell of flowers; instead He has allowed crooked trees to fit suitably into a wood, grey clouds to provide the right sort of contrast in the heavens, strange and unmusical notes to make up the complete orchestration of nature. Why not, then, human misfits as well?

"That may be all very well", comes the ready comment, "from God's point of view, and it may even indicate the line which we should take when dealing with tiresome and rest-

less people; but what about the misfit himself? If he is con-
stitutionally unable to make himself at home anywhere, he is
surely wanting in a quality which is due to his human nature." He may be so wanting—if you consider the facility for
striking roots to be *due* to human nature—but the more important point is that the individual is created for an individual
purpose, and if certain elements of normal humanity are left
out so as to make room for others which are more valuable,
then God is not above substituting the greater for the less.
Admittedly restlessness is not a good thing in itself; admittedly to be able to settle down in life is a natural advantage
to which man normally has a right; allowing for all this it is
now surely a question of relative values taking their place in
the scale. If dependence on God is more likely to be developed in any given soul by keeping him unanchored and full
of longings which are to continue unsatisfied, then why not
deprive him of a good which to the generality of mankind
is a more or less necessary adjunct to sanctification?

Certainly in the history of sanctity there is evidence of
what might be called the vocation of the missed vocation.
There are souls, that is, who feel themselves cut out by nature and grace for one particular kind of work for God and
yet who find themselves eventually doing, under obedience
or by force of circumstance, something quite different. Little to show for what was originally their "vocation": blocked
at every turn they spend their lives questing, groping, starting and never being able to finish, trying one thing after another and everything without success . . . driftwood. Like
stranded trippers who have lost their return ticket they are
for ever looking for lodgings . . . and for ever having to
sleep in shelters along the sea front.

Unstable they may be, but do not tell me that such souls
are neurotics or that they are necessarily being unfaithful to
grace. How can we be sure that God wants them to find
permanent, or even temporary, lodging? How do we know
that God did not let them lose one ticket so that they might
find another? Might not such souls be just the kind who, if
they were established in a work where they felt themselves

to be secure, would settle down too much and become smug? To be self-sufficient, no longer to look for the day-to-day revelation of God's will, is far worse than being restless. Restlessness can be one of the by-products of hungering and thirsting after justice. St. Augustine confessed his interior restlessness. It is implicit in the yearnings of all who fall in love with God. In lesser men it may express itself in a natural craving for change; in the more generous it takes the form of a supernatural, and patient, craving for security in God. In most men it is a mixture of the two. No blame to them. They might do worse.

A NOTE ON PRAYER

The reason why nothing about prayer has yet been said in this book is that so much has already been said in the earlier volumes of the series. Since, however, prayer of one sort or another is the highest act which man can perform on earth no discussion of the subject can ever be really redundant. Be that as it may, prayer is going to be discussed here.

There, unfortunately, lies much of the trouble: discussion of a subject can take the place of the subject itself. Just as we can talk about prayer and not pray, so *in* our prayer we can think about prayer and not pray. Apart from deliberate distractions and discouragement, the main obstacle to true interior prayer is thought about true interior prayer.

To think about prayer is to think about how I am praying. Self becomes, if not the object, at least the focus point. Whereas to pray properly is to leave self and to love God.

We excuse ourselves for this mania for self-analysis and prayer-analysis and method-analysis on the grounds that the exercise of worship is vitally important and that we must therefore get it right. We must take it to bits, oil it, put it together again. Why must we? For the sake of the prayer? For the sake of our own peace of mind? For the sake of God? On each of these counts we should rather leave prayer to

God's valuation than try and find a workable system of measurement. People do not overhaul a radio for the sake of the radio but for the sake of the sound. The sound, in the case of prayer, can be heard by God alone. The process of overhauling is liable to become a mere hobby, an interest for itself's sake. It is also a suspension of valuable time when the sound might be going up to God.

Because prayer escapes measurement, and because even the book of instructions is unable to guarantee success, people give up trying to pray. What it really means is that people have only the haziest notion of what is wanted of the soul in prayer. They read about the mechanism of prayer and are either put off by its complexities or else genuinely unable to trace any relation between what they see in the book and what they experience in their own souls. They see devotion in others, they vaguely remember devotion in themselves; they expect warmth and clarity and neatness, but find only coldness and fog and untidiness; they believe that prayer is a vital force in the world, they wish that the world would turn to prayer, they envy those who have the gift for it . . . but they cannot give more than a notional assent to the truth that they personally are meant to practise it. Again let it be said that the reason why everything in their experience seems to convince such souls that they cannot pray is simply that they do not know what they are expected to be giving to God in their prayer.

Now in prayer the soul both gives something of itself to God and gets something of God in return. The more the soul gives of itself the more, obviously, does God communicate Himself to the soul. But the proportion received on either side, God's or the soul's, cannot possibly be estimated. We, accustomed to material systems of exchange, look for parallel systems in the spiritual order. And are consequently disappointed. For example when we enter a shop we do so with certain assumptions in mind: we are prepared to pay, we expect to be served with what we are asking for, we will take our custom elsewhere if our needs are not catered for. Years of this sort of thing induce the shopping mentality with regard to prayer. Approaching it with the same assumptions with which we approach our shopping list, and treating God as we would treat a shopkeeper who possessed an infinite store of goods, we cannot accordingly see why, provided we are ready to pay the price, we should not be served with what we want. "We won't shop here any more," we say. "It isn't any good."

The confusion is twofold: we have mistaken the nature of the goods, and we are offering payment in the wrong sort of currency. So of course, puzzled, we leave the shop. The two things which we have to learn, then, are: first, that what God has in store is not necessarily what has attracted us in the shop window but something far more worth having; second, that the retail price is not the figure we see on the label—the cost to us is one of faith. Prayer, we must realise, is conditioned by faith: we have to believe that God is ready to do business with us at all times; equally we have to go on trusting that He knows best when He asks of us a prayer which defeats our systems of accountancy. Faith and perseverance are the absolute essentials: there can be no discount here.

A PRAYER WHICH *IS* HEARD

"Until now, you have not been making any requests in my name; make them and they will be granted, to bring you gladness in full measure." We read these words of our Lord in John's sixteenth chapter, and at once begin to wonder what we can ask for. "Happiness," we say, "let us ask for that . . . He has promised to bring us gladness in full measure . . . let us see if He brings it." In praying for this gladness, there is one thing to be taken into account—namely that our idea of it must tally with that which exists in the mind of God.

Everyone has his picture of happiness. To one it means sitting under a tree on summer evenings with the bees humming in the honeysuckle and a dog resting against one's legs; to another it means snow and a mountain; to another the delights of art or abstract thought or the company of friends. Is it one of these things which we are praying for? If it is, how can we be sure that we shall be in the right mood for it when our prayer comes to be heard? Because not only has everyone got a different picture of happiness but everyone has a different way of looking at it when it comes along. Our ideas about it change because our moods regarding its accidentals change. Sometimes we are afraid that our ideas may change too much and that we shall be cheated of what we now want. But, of course, the real danger is not that our view of happiness may change too much but that it will not change enough. Happiness is meant to lead us up the scale until we want only what God wants and because He wants it.

Happiness, then, is not a matter of having a dream and working round towards its realisation; it is much more a matter of being in tune. Not so much of forcing reality out of a dream, but of finding idealism in actuality. For instance, we may look forward for years to a certain setting in which our believed happiness is to be fulfilled, we may manœuvre ourselves into all the right positions, we may actually achieve the results which we have seen so clearly on paper, and yet find that there is no relation between ourselves and our dreamt-of happiness. We are somehow not in the mood. The effort has been wasted. Our own and other people's lives have been disturbed, and there is nothing worth while to show for it all. It is because we have mistaken the outward for the inward. The outward may certainly have a good deal to do with it, but the essential element of happiness is one of relationship—the link between the mind and the material which lies to hand. It is an adjustment of the spirit and not a disposition of circumstances. Only in the mind can relationships be established: circumstances cannot establish anything so subtle as happiness, they can only surround.

The confusion is due to the misleading behaviour of the soul's lower faculties, memory and imagination. The soul, remembering a time of happiness, confuses the scene with the substance. It imagines that the same juxtapositions must produce the same state. "Give me another summer like the last one and I shall be happy again." You won't be unless it is the kind which you can carry with you into the winter. Give me, give me, give me. . . . If we identify happiness with having what we want, we should not complain if God does not hear our prayer for it.

The moral of all this is to try not to allow our view of happiness to be coloured by what memory and imagination tell us about it. They are nearly always wrong. They paint for us a disposition which may or may not be capable of realisation, and then suggest that we should clap it onto an existing set-up. Whereas if the will does not elicit dispositions from the existing set-up, nothing will emerge at all. Happiness comes up from inside, it is not something superimposed. Dispositions are not projectable or transferable or predictable.

"I don't see why I should blindfold myself in this way," it might be objected, "for according to you I must exercise no choice in the matter. It seems I have to be passive with regard to happiness, accepting it if it comes along but making no move in the direction where I feel it to be. Surely man has a right to his happiness, and if he has any sense he will know where his particular happiness is to be found." Some of this is true; most of it is false. In the first place who ever said we had a *right* to happiness? We have a natural appetite for it, and we have every reason to hope that a taste of it may be given us, but so far as *this* life goes we have no absolute claim. In fact no claim whatever. There is a lot too much talk about being entitled to one's share of happiness—as if we had God in our debt. "I don't guarantee to make you happy on earth," said our Lady to Bernadette . . . and the implications are obvious.

What then of the text from St. John? What of this gladness which Christ comes to bring? Surely the answer is that the only gladness which is really worth having is that which arises from doing God's will. If you say that this is not the sort of gladness you want, then you must know that you are wanting the wrong sort of gladness . . . and have never experienced the right one. This is certainly the kind which we may request in His name, knowing that He will grant it in full measure.

If God does not grant us the answer to our prayer, it is often because He has already granted us the gladness and we have not recognised it. We have got a cheque in our pocket and we are moaning about our lack of gold and silver. If we refuse to cash the cheque, we *are* poor. If we refuse to take up the happiness which God is ready to let us have, we naturally have to get along as best we can on the concepts of happiness which we have formed for ourselves—with a consequent sense of insufficiency. How can our pathetic little structure of personal contentment, our happiness of comfort, our greedy counterfeits and furtive pleasures do duty for what might be ours? The kind of happiness which we are left with is nothing but unhappiness under another name. "How often have I been ready to gather thy children together as a hen gathers her chickens under her wings; and thou wouldst not. Behold, your house is left to you desolate." That is the reason why we are desolate: we prefer our own shelter.

RESPONSIBILITY

Not everyone shrinks from responsibility. There are those who perhaps do not shrink from it enough. What follows is intended to show that responsibility can be one of the most direct and effective means of sanctification. It is one thing to shrink and yet take it on because you have to, and another to shrink and evade it because you are lazy or afraid.

Taken in the wrong way responsibility may lead to a variety of excesses: on the one side arrogance, pomposity, hardness, assumption of infallibility, ambition; scrupulosity, pettiness, jealousy, suspicion and dread on the other. Taken in the right way it leads to dependence upon God. "Cast all your care on God, for He has care of you" is the text for the soul who puts his responsibility on a supernatural basis. The soul who takes the material view has in mind either personal power or, reasonably enough under the circumstances, desire to escape.

Responsibility, like obedience of which it is an offshoot, de-

rives from God. It must therefore be referred back again to
God. Once this essential fact is grasped, there is nothing more
to worry about. God looks after His own. A spiritual man
makes a muddle of his opportunities only when he is opportunist in his approach to them. If he takes upon his shoulders
the full responsibility, leaving God out of the picture, then
obviously he is left by God with the full responsibility. He
then gets along without the assistance of grace. Is it surprising
that so many of our self-appointed enterprises fail? The weight
of responsibility is an imponderable. Only when we have committed its burdens to Divine Providence, from whom they
came, are we safe against having taken on more than we
bargained for.

Those others, the people who wriggle away from the obligations which life imposes, are doomed to a course of one
flight after another. They will always find themselves being
faced with decisions to be made and policies to be pursued;
and unless they take up these repeated challenges they will
go on hedging and flitting until there is no sort of stability
left in their characters. Indecision whittles away the supports
of the will; and fickleness, doubt, reflex examinations, defeatism are the result.

There was once a monk who believed himself to be so much
devoted to the virtue of holy obedience that in the end he
never made up his mind about anything. He would run to his
superior and ask whether he was to drink tea or coffee at
breakfast. The superior, for his part, was ready enough to
make whatever decisions were necessary—though some of the
requests must have tried his patience sorely. Although it was
the superior's duty to shoulder responsibility, it was also his
duty to form his subjects in responsibility. It would seem
therefore that in this particular case the superior was more
irresponsible than the subject. If Heli's sons were lacking in a
sense of responsibility, so also was Heli.

It is the fault particularly of religious people that they
hand over to others, on the grounds that their own judgement
is imperfect, the duty of making a choice. This is far less
meritorious than it looks. It is often sheer laziness and cow-

ardice. Advice should be sought in order to assist decision, not take the place of it. Again and again we find on looking back that we have made mistakes because we have listened too much to the opinions of our friends. It is we who are to blame, not they. We were too ready, evidently, to lean. We may ask for information and we may ask for a ruling: the doubt in both cases has to do with a fact. Advice has not to do with facts but with choices. We have no business to ask for advice unless we retain the right—sometimes a very painful right— to choose. The mere fact of being in doubt as to how we should act does not absolve us from further responsibility: the choice does not henceforth rest with another. All that the other can do is to clear our minds, help us to make them up, say what *he* would do if he were us. We still have the responsibility of being ourselves. It is we who shall be judged for the choices which we make, and it is idle to imagine that anyone else in the world can do what God specifically wants of us.

DISINTERESTEDNESS

Following what has been said on the subject of responsibility, the question arises as to how far disinterestedness is a virtue and how far it is an evasion. Am I, by holding myself aloof from the affairs of men, refusing my share of life's burdens . . . or am I revealing an admirable detachment? Am I self-ishly insulating myself against mankind . . . or paying it the compliment of minding my own business? Different schools of thought would give different answers. The question is a wide one. So wide, indeed, that the relative value of the active and the contemplative vocation comes within its scope. Thus whatever the ideas which will be suggested in this section, an exact dividing line between the right and the wrong kind of indifference can hardly be expected. In a matter which has to make allowance for individual calls it would be rash to generalise.

A man should be sufficiently disinterested to be able to see life apart from the *solatia* attaching to any one particular life. That is to say he should be above making the perquisites his main reason for undertaking anything. This is not high sanctity: it is common sense. To consider the luxuries while ignoring the essentials is to ask for future disillusion. It is of the first importance to be able to distinguish between what is of the margin of life and what is of the life itself. For high sanctity you need something else: you need to eliminate the margin.

If being disinterested is to mean more than merely being not interested, it has to be an offshoot of humility. People who are really humble can afford to be supremely unconcerned about many of the things which upset the proud. The humble man does not bother about what others are saying of him, does not waste time in trying to create an impression, does not scheme for positions, does not suspect other people's motives, does not worry when he cannot get what he wants, does not go in for spite or a desire for revenge. In fact the humble man is spared a good deal.

The problem for the truly disinterested is not how to curb their curiosity but how to express their zeal. They are on fire with charity, while at the same time being aware of what a danger to charity is the useless spending of self. Wanting to benefit mankind, they know that they can do so only in proportion as they do not want to benefit themselves. It is not easy to give without thought of reward. Nor does mankind help in the process: mankind is sometimes so overwhelmingly grateful.

Many a would-be apostle has started off with the best intentions, and then has been side-tracked in his apostolate. He has hated worldliness, he has avoided publicity, he has worked himself to the bone, he has launched movements, given excellent advice, won the admiration of his followers, died in harness and respected by all . . . and yet been a complete failure. Why is it that such people are not saints? What is it that prevents all that excellent zeal from being of any real supernatural value? Why are such people forgotten, together with their work, ten years after their death? The answer is simply that they have not been sufficiently disinterested. They may not have wanted money or reputation or applause, but they certainly wanted something. The tragedy is that if we go on wanting something badly enough, God lets us have it.

For the soul who aims at serving God with any sort of real perfection, there must be detachment not only from the more obviously accidental acquisitions of life but from the more interior ones as well. A spiritual person must train himself to do without spiritual satisfaction. The sense of achievement is the most difficult of the senses to mortify, but if disinterestedness means anything it means denying the appetite for vain glory. For purposes of contemplation disinterestedness must mean not only the readiness to mind one's own business but also the readiness not to mind one's own business too much. The spiritual man must be indifferent to the stages of his progress. Once he has got the direction right, and the will to go along it at all costs, he must be prepared to leave the pace and the ordering of his journey to God. This is spiritual disinterestedness, and far harder to acquire than the other.

HOW DOES THIS WORK OUT?

It might justifiably be said that all this talk about responsibility and detachment gets us, in actual practice, nowhere. The one, it might be suggested, cancels the other out. "What we want to know," says the plain blunt man, "is this: when do we go out and work for souls, and when do we stop at home and pray for them?" You want to know, in other words, what exactly the obligation of charity amounts to. The answer is given by our Lord: we have to love God with the whole heart, and our neighbour as ourselves. If we really grasp what this means we see the relation between action and contemplation, between responsibility towards mankind and detachment from the concerns of men. But in order to grasp

the meaning of the proposition we need to do more than look
at the significance of the words: we need to be living the life.
The confusion of loyalties exists only because the life of charity is not fully taken on. Where it is fully taken on, as for instance it is by the saints, the obligation is seen not as two
expressions but as one. By withdrawing from creatures the
soul helps the world outside himself; by giving himself to the
service of men the soul grows in interior charity.

Taking the first clause of the gospel precept, we see that it
is only by being entrenched in the love of God that we can
begin to understand what is meant by the love of anything
else. When a soul loves God with the whole heart he finds
suddenly that there is room in it for the whole world. Logi-
cally and chronologically the first clause comes first. Hence
St. Augustine's often misinterpreted saying: "love God and do
what you will." Given the complete surrender of the affections
and the will to God, the soul is not likely to make a mistake
in spending itself on one aspect of charity at the expense of
the other. The reason for this is that there is no obstacle to
the influx of light. In the measure that the soul is emptied of
self, God is able to make His directives clear. He may urge a
deeper withdrawal from outward contacts or He may incline
the soul to greater activity. He may call for both at different
times. The point is that if the soul really loves God it does not
matter which vocation is being followed at the moment. Each
is equally fruitful because it is not the soul's work which is
being done, but God's. Activity which comes from a soul that
is selfless and wholly dedicated to God is necessarily the work
of grace. The charity is equally pure whether it is directed
towards other souls or, more immediately, towards God.

From this it follows that the second clause of the gospel
precept is an amplification of the first. Loving God, the soul
must perforce love those whom God loves. And when we ask
how this love is to be expressed we find that the answer is
within our own selves: we must work to obtain outwardly for
others what inwardly we desire as the good towards which
we tend. The standard is there, is absolute, is measurable. It
gives us, always provided that the first clause is established,

the light we need. It may involve us in distraction, in risk, in suffering and in every sort of unforeseen eventuality, but so long as our wills retain their disinterestedness and do not attempt to reclaim the love which has been given to God, it cannot involve us in spiritual loss. Feeling bewildered and even unsettled by a life in which a new range of responsibilities declares itself does not—although the disturbance may amount to an agony verging almost on despair—disprove the supernatural purpose of the thing. On the contrary, it verifies it.

The practical question—namely whether this particular course of action does or does not take me away from God—is not so difficult to resolve as people think. It becomes difficult only when personal interests are consulted instead of God's. The moment the soul says "what would *I* like?", a fog begins to spread over the horizon, and the chances are all against making a right decision. The only way to ensure clarity in this kind of doubt is to stand aside and judge the thing as far as possible apart from the feelings. Once the soul is determined to follow God's will in spite of either scruples or hardship or distraction or prejudice, *then* almost always comes the light, and the courage, to move. Having moved, the rightness or wrongness of the decision can be determined by its effects. Not, needless to say, by the outward success of the action, but by the repercussions which it has upon the interior life. For example the action stands condemned at once if pride or obstinacy or uncharity results. In the case of religious there are additional tests to be found in how far the undertaking is wished by superiors, how far it reflects the spirit of the particular order, how far it suits or inconveniences the other members of the community.

If a man is honest with himself he is not likely to be dishonest with God. If, that is, he can frankly pin down his motive and determine what really is his desire he will be able to regulate his measure of activity with sufficient accuracy. The whole thing, in the last analysis, lies in the desire. Where shallow minds will see success in spectacular achievements, judging that certain lines of activity must inevitably be justified if certain results are produced, spiritually orientated souls will look only at the desire which gives to the effort its direction. If the desire cannot be estimated, the work is not estimated either. Thus it would be the greatest mistake either to condemn or applaud the decision of any individual, however reputedly "interior", who should associate himself with works of zeal. Few are in a position to know his desire. All things being equal, which they very seldom are, it would be safer for the interior man not to mount the platform, not to write to the papers, not to grasp the microphone or volunteer to sit on committees, but at the same time it would be rash to assume that his impulse was selfish: he may be acting on the impulse of grace: he may have sifted his desires and directed his intention solely towards God: his feelings in the matter need not be considered either way.

In her *Dialogues* St. Catherine records how God told her: "No virtue can merit eternal life for you if you serve me in a finite manner, for I, the infinite God, wish to be served in an infinite manner, and you have nothing approaching the infinite save the desire and the transports of your soul." Whatever is accomplished independently of God has, for the spiritual man, an ephemeral value only: it is a vulgarity, a departure, a strident proclamation of personal vanity. The same work, performed in what St. Catherine calls the infinite manner, may be an achievement of the highest sanctity. Useless, then, to measure any enterprise except by the standard of spiritual aspiration. And if this is very often hidden from the person most concerned, it is all the more hidden from those who judge by what they see.

THE MORE SUBTLE DETACHMENT

From what has been said in the foregoing sections it may be deduced that detachment does not end with indifference to material gain or to the claims of self-will in outward action: the implications are more far-reaching and include indifference to spiritual benefits. John Tauler, who is one of the most uncompromising apostles of detachment, is emphatic about the necessity of interior detachment before all other. "To die completely to all interior enjoyment" is the demand which he makes in one of his sermons for Pentecost. The only way, he tells us, to avoid getting caught up in sidetracking motives is "to be renewed by spiritual desires, by fervent prayers to our Lord. That is how we can be born again in Christ, and without it we cannot be pleasing to Him." Thus it is no good our wanting more of contemplation than God wants to let us have. To do so is nothing more than to want our kind of contemplation, not His . . . to want His gift and not His will. It is, ultimately, to want ourselves and not God. The bottom has fallen out of detachment here, and we are back again at vulgar greed.

Spiritual people are liable to get all this wrong precisely because they *are* spiritual people: that is because they are labelled spiritual, because they have no worldly ambitions, because their whole interest is directed towards God. Such souls imagine that the more they hunger after spirituality—seen in their terms—the better. So they go on hungering and stimulating the appetite. All this means is that they are dragging inward things into the open and lining them up with the material things which they have renounced. They are being less consistent, and spiritually less detached, than the confessed materialist.

"True abstraction," says Tauler, "is the quality that makes a soul withdraw from everything and turn away from all that is not exclusively God. It is that which makes one examine all one's words and deeds, all one's thoughts with clear judgement to see if in one's heart there is anything hidden which is not of God . . . and if one should find oneself seeking anything else but God it must be excluded, rejected and cut off." The great Dominican goes on to say that in spite of the grimness of this doctrine it is the certain way to peace. How could it be anything else? Detachment from material conceptions of the spiritual life must inevitably produce in the soul the same liberty which, on a lower plane, results from indifference to physical discomfort and luxury. The detached soul is borne along by grace.

Such detachment as we are considering here is not likely to come about unless the whole business of the life of faith is taken on without reservation. It is not merely a question of making a resolution to deny oneself the effort to find sweetness in prayer. This would be easy enough. True detachment is the outcome of the life of faith. It is the gradual substitution of new values for old, it is the habit of mind which sees spirituality from God's point of view instead of from man's, it results in a refusal to be either dazzled or discouraged by symbols, forms, signs, accidentals of any sort. The truly interior soul does not depend upon interior experiences any more than upon exterior comforts. The emotions are seen to be just as natural as all other created satisfactions. The peace which is now sought for is the peace which comes of being able to do without peace. Prayer is practised without self-questioning. Penance is no longer clung to as an agreeable sop to one's conscience, but practised objectively as an expression of love. Work, activity, suffering, obedience, the virtues and obligations of one's state are all so many responses to the inspiration of grace. Nothing is departmental any longer: all is covered by the demand of God.

So long as the soul is concerned about what it feels like to respond to God there is a want of perfect detachment. The full response is above disappointment and congratulation. The full response envisages nothing but the naked will of God. Souls who mistake the will of God for something else, souls who fail in their service and spend their lives in a sterile dream, souls who appear to have the best intentions but who never seem to be able to do either themselves or other people any good, are nearly always those who have become inordinately attached to an idea. Had the attachment been to a possession or to a person it would have been broken long ago. But because it was to a way of praying or to a conception of sanctity or to a mistaken loyalty, it has escaped the ruthless abnegation which it has deserved. Ideas are not only more subtle than possessions and people, but they cling closer. They are ourselves. But we have to be detached from ourselves.

PEACE IN GOD

You cannot discuss peace without discussing war. Not that peace is the absence of war—or it would be something negative and not a quality in its own right—but that peace is fully appreciated only in contrast to its opposite. Turning from the temporal to the spiritual order we see that peace is understood to mean more than either absence of disturbance or enjoyment of sensible security. The peace of faith is something deeper than tranquillity as opposed to disorder and trouble: it is tranquillity *in* disorder and trouble. Indeed disturbance might almost be claimed as one of the conditions of peace in God; certainly it is a test of its purity and perfection. Perhaps this is why disturbance, both inward and outward, is the setting in which most contemplative souls are called upon to lead their lives.

Now if interior peace is not something more than an interlude between interior upsets, it is nothing much more than exterior peace. True peace is a habit, not a lull. It is a lasting trust, not a period of relief or reaction, not a spasm. The sense of rest need not enter into it at all: true peace is not a sense, it is a fact. Before going any further we must examine the supposed opposite quality to interior peace, and see then whether the two can exist at the same time in the one soul.

Take the extreme case: the desolation which is called the dark night of the spirit. Here is a warfare, a confusion, a disturbance in which there is nothing perceptibly peaceful whatever. The soul is so busy appreciating its distress that there can be no *sense* of security. The security is there right enough, but it is one of obscure faith and not of emotion. Nor is this desolation confined to the times when the soul happens to be engaged in prayer. Indeed experience seems to show that most contemplative souls are, at this particular stage in the spiritual life, less aware of their misery when praying than when not. At least while actually in prayer there is the sense of trying, however hopelessly, to do something worth while. During the rest of the day there is a sense of complete futility.

The interior destitution which is suffered by certain contemplative souls is such that they begin the day with loathing and dread, praying for the strength which will enable them to get through their waking hours, and end it with the satisfaction of knowing that they are now one day nearer their release. The condition is one of almost unbroken hate. Not that this hatred is ever extended to people, or even that it shows itself. It is a hatred of minutes. There is a fierce shrinking from the future, there is a thorough detestation of the present, and, though it is known to be idle, there is a lonely regret about the past. God is felt to be miles away, work is distasteful and resorted to with the guilty feeling that it is being used as an escape, people are either a weariness or else a source of misgiving and temptation. Such is roughly the picture. Yet in the midst of all this it is possible to preserve the true peace of which we speak. It is the peace of acceptance.

In the light of the above we can see what a gulf must exist between the peace which the world offers and the peace which the spirit sometimes exacts. But this secret peace is no mere fiction as some might be led, from the above account, to suppose: the fact that it is a reality may be judged only by living the life of faith. From the initial act of surrender to the ordinance of God, from having taken on whatever destitution of spirit God may choose to allow, the soul finds increasingly as fresh problems come along, and as the ways of the interior life are travelled, that nothing can now surprise it into any sort of real rebellion of the will. There may be mistakes, but there are no deliberate resentments or infidelities. The soul has come to terms with suffering.

And this is peace. Here at last is a balance which cannot be seriously upset.

The secret of peace, then, is co-operation. When the powers of the soul are in harmony with the will of God there is no room for what is not peace. There is room for sorrow, for outward failure, for fear and loneliness and doubt. But there is no room for war. War in the soul is possible only where there is resistance. Resistance militates not only against the possibility of peace but also against the chances of happiness. Happiness and peace are not the same thing. The spiritual life does not pledge itself to procure human happiness; it does pledge itself to procure interior peace. Peace, the kind discussed here, is more important than happiness. It often leads to happiness. Happiness does not always —though it does sometimes—lead to peace.

ORDEAL BY FIRE

We have seen something of the process by which the imperfections of the soul are burned away—spiritual desolation being as it were the appropriate blow-lamp. Here we examine further some of the characteristics of this divine heat, noting a few points of conduct to be observed while in the flame.

The action of grace consumes self in such a way that, throwing to the surface all the evil which has been more or less hidden in the depths for years, the soul sees its own beastliness as never before. It sees how smug it has been in its sheltered spirituality, how blind to reality, how ready it has been to put on an act which has deceived everyone else as well as itself. The soul experiences now the bitterness of disillusion. The whole horizon is filled with its sin. Not any one sin, but all sin: the horizon shows unrelieved self. The mistake which the soul is now likely to make is that of imagining this to be the whole picture. It cannot distinguish between the real and the accidental self: sin and self are identified in the mind. Such a misconception can bring a soul perilously close to despair. The true self stands apart from all this firework display which so disgusts its spiritual sensibilities. It is too much to expect the soul to appreciate this—indeed the force of the particular trial would be lost if it did—but so far as conduct goes it is to be acted upon. To do so is one of the conditions of the life of faith.

Disgust and unquiet, then, are necessary factors in the burning process of purification: disgust must be there so as to separate the essential from the accidental; disquiet must be there so as to elicit the act of trust. The surrender would be incomplete without these two elements. The state is well described by Père de Langeac:[1] "Darkness envelops her, the waves of bitterness rise up to her lips. It seems to her that her happiness has only been a dream. All within her appears to be ugly and spoilt. Nothing is pure in her eyes. Who knows if she will ever taste again the joys of happy days? They are now so far away, and the evil is present, so real, so universal, so tenacious, so deep. No doubt there remains in the soul, in the depths of herself, a secret hope, but so feeble that she hardly dares believe it."

The trial is a particularly lonely one because nobody else can appreciate the reality of the suffering or bring any sort of lasting encouragement. The ordinary friends to whom the soul might reasonably turn for understanding see only failure, self-pity, and weakness. This is not altogether their fault: it is simply that they judge by the same evidence as the soul judges by, and though they are faced with far less of it they conclude that there has been a falling-off. Now this is quite as it should be: the beauty with which the soul is being clothed must, for the time being and until the perfection has become a habit, be secret. When the operation of grace has established the soul in a settled way of holiness there will not be the same need for concealment. By then there will be humility in the soul, by then there will be trust: the good opinions of others will no longer act as a threat to the action

[1] In his *Vie cachée en Dieu.*

of the spirit. But until then others, as well as the soul itself, must be kept in the dark. "Despoiled of all which was her apparent riches," says the author just quoted, "the interior soul has begun to be renewed with the beauty of God."

Even the director can, at this stage, bring little enough help. Though, unlike the others who see what is outward and so draw the wrong conclusions, he may know the course which grace is taking in the soul, he is debarred, and knows himself to be debarred, from making any impression. The relationship between the two becomes simply one of confessor and penitent: both realising that the situation has gone beyond the point where advice is going to be of any use. Absolution is as much needed as ever, but apart from practical directives regarding conduct there is nothing to be done or asked for. It is now for the soul to hang on and resist the temptation to despair, and for the director to avoid tying up his penitent in knots of multiplicity or false hope. Directors have an unfortunate way, prompted by genuine sympathy, of prophesying the finish of these nights. This is a rash thing to do because souls have been known to burn away in the darkness for years, and their burning is all the harder to bear if their expectations are for ever being disappointed. Faith is difficult enough as it is, and if belief in the wisdom of a director is nibbled away by the evidence of miscalculations it becomes more of a strain than it is intended to be.

CONSEQUENCES OF THIS ORDEAL

The primary reason for the sense of destitution and near-despair is, as we have seen, that the act of trust should be elicited. But there is another reason for it as well, a reason which is not so generally appreciated. It is in order to continue in the individual soul the redemptive work of Christ. This second reason is developed by L. M. Cautheron in *Valeur apostolique de la vie contemplative* and is worth quoting here. "One of the principal means by which God uses such a soul for others is found in the sense of identification with sinners in the way that our Lord allowed His innocence to be identified with iniquity. Thus the contemplative is able in his solitude and depths of weakness and imperfection to fill up that which is wanting in the Passion of Christ for His Body which is the Church." This is vastly significant. It means that the very evil which the soul sees in itself during this ordeal may be turned into good. Not merely put up with and so, indirectly, made material for patience. Much more immediately its acknowledged existence is, by the alchemy of Christ's sufferings, made positively sanctifying. It is almost as if Christ, by becoming "sin" for man, picks up man's "sin" and makes an offering of it to the Father. Not that evil can ever be presented as good—this would be a contradiction which heretics would make use of at once—but that the weakness and even corruption which the action of grace discovers to the soul is, in virtue of what Christ took upon Himself when assuming the responsibility of man's guilt, made the occasion of furthering Christ's work for souls. The sin itself does not further Christ's work: what furthers Christ's work is the pain of seeing the sinfulness in the soul. It is not a question here of good coming out of evil; it is rather a question of so hating the evil that the suffering which results is good. It is meritorious. The soul is granted a share in the Agony. As Christ in the Garden shrank with loathing from the iniquity of man, so the soul shrinks from its own defilement and thus is allowed to co-operate in Christ's prayer for the world. "In those flames the contemplative must be purified," writes Gautheron, "and because he is willing to pass through this fire of purification the contemplative has the power of giving love to the rest of men."

In the light of the above it is easy to see our Lady's place in the apostolic work of the Church. As Mother of Sorrows she is the first preacher of her Son's Gospel. Seeing the sinfulness of man more clearly than any other apostle she has proportionately more power of giving love to the world. Hers is essentially the mission of the suffering contemplative. Immeasurably more fruitful, then, is a soul's purification by this ordeal of fire than any active work for souls to which his zeal may incline him. Where Christ and Mary saw sin outside themselves and suffered its weight upon their souls, the contemplative sees sin within as well as without . . . and, bowing to the pain of it, finds a place in their redemptive love.

The particular kind of apostolate here discussed is one which has to be handled carefully. Slightly misconceived, the doctrine is open to serious error. It would be possible, for example, to delude oneself into the belief that one's imperfections should not only be seen but also, in order to be fully purifying, be accepted and consented to. Temptation would thus be looked upon as a good in itself. Whereas temptation, evil of any sort, can be purifying only in so far as it rouses an effective opposition in the will. Precisely because in the interior soul the opposition is so strong, precisely because the presence of temptation is so vivid and agonising, does this sort of apostolate acquire its value. If there were no refusal to capitulate there would be no battle. If there were no battle there would be no grief. The sorrows of the interior soul are a consequence, not a cause. If we are looking for causes we find them in the conflicts between nature and grace. Suffering is simply the effect, the necessary price which the soul has to pay, for its purification and its apostolate.

Moreover, though this is perhaps here by the way, it is the preparation for a grace which God, when dealing with such souls, normally has in store. The suffering disposes the soul for what the authorities call the grace of transforming union. If and when this culmination is realised there will be no longer the same conflicts between nature and grace: self will have submitted entirely to God. The human will is then united with the divine. Where the surrender is absolute there can be no disturbance, no sense of rebellion. The trials, though spiritual, must be now of another order: they cannot constitute interior upheavals such as we have been considering.

To conclude. By waiting, trusting, suspending the natural

tendency towards self-condemnation in the face of what appears to be irrefutable evidence, the soul both benefits itself and communicates love to others. To do anything else is to hinder the operation of grace. Union with God and union with the members of Christ's mystical body must develop more surely by this than by any other way. It is the acid test of progress. It is the culmination of the law of love. It is the life of faith. Accept this and you advance, refuse it and you go back. Of course it means darkness, disappointment, misgiving. Only along such lines can contemplative souls impart spirituality to others: the supernatural life is communicated in the way that Christ communicates it to the Church. The Church is Christ, is the supernatural life. As the Father creates, as the Son redeems, as the Spirit sanctifies, so, on his finite plane, the soul of man imparts the spiritual gifts he has received. "In the manner by which the Father is related to the Son by communication, and the Son to the Holy Ghost," writes de Langeac,[1] "so are interior souls related to one another and to mankind. Nature does not enter into this mode of communication: that which is born of the spirit is spirit . . . and must remain so."

CONTEMPLATION AS AN APOSTOLATE

The apostolic life is higher than any other, says St. Thomas, because it is the perfection of the contemplative life. It is not higher, directly, because it is the most selfless. Still less is it higher because it gets the most done. It is higher because it derives its force, and in proportion as it derives its force, from prayer. "Those whose earnest zeal and fervour vow them to prayer and penance contribute more to the progress of the Church than the active workers in the Lord's field," we read in the encyclical *Umbratilem,* "for if the former did

[1] Though this is quoted from notes and not from the text of his *Vie cachée en Dieu.*

not obtain from heaven an abundance of divine grace to water the fields, the evangelical workers would reap but a scanty harvest." This quotation should be enough to silence for ever those who say that enclosed orders are no longer any use in the world of today and that souls do far more for the Church by going out and working among men.

The case which is made out for contemplative communities is usually based on the experience of history. Thus for instance it is pointed out that had St. Teresa of Lisieux joined an active order she would have influenced only an immediate circle and her work would have died with her. As it was, from the obscurity of Carmel, she influenced and continues to influence thousands upon thousands. Her autobiography has been translated into more languages than the plays of Mr. Bernard Shaw or the speeches of Mr. Churchill. This argument is valid enough as far as it goes, but it does not, of course, account for the numberless souls who live and die in Carmel and who do not write autobiographies. The sceptical critic will not be convinced when you tell him that it was St. Teresa's hidden life which gave value to her written work, and that what she was doing by way of silent contemplation and secret penance is much what innumerable other nuns were doing as well. You may tell him that God from time to time draws a contemplative into the limelight so as to stress the need for contemplation in the world, and that even if He did not, *the very fact* of souls giving themselves to Him in the withdrawn life of love has a leavening effect upon mankind at large . . . you may tell him this, and your sceptic will ask for further proof. The argument is one which takes you all the way only if you are prepared to go all the way with it.

A different approach to the question would be through the purpose of man and the nature of prayer itself. However doubtful the layman may be about the value of the contemplative life he must, if he is a believer at all and still more if he is a Catholic, accept the fact that man is made for God, and that prayer, in the widest sense, is the channel of correspondence. If union with God is the end of man, and if relationship can be established by means of receiving grace from God in prayer and giving in return the direction of human life by prayer, then both the purer the prayer and the more it is practised the better. This is just as true in the case of mankind at large as it is in the case of the individual. Consequently if the majority of men neglect prayer it falls to the minority to make good the defect. The world benefits when people make it their whole business to pray. The contemplative vocation is not a loss to the active life: it is its support. Leaving the world, souls help the world. The principle may be pressed further, and it can be claimed that if contemplation were to die out there would be nothing to keep religion from secularisation. Love is a unity, and if contemplative love were drained away active love would follow suit. If the mystical body is to be healthy, if it is to remain capable of movement, if it is to live and not merely exist, there must be at least as much energy in the interior faculties as there is in the external limbs.

The mistake which the world makes is to judge of intensity as well as of utility by visible achievement. The very serenity which is to some the best recommendation of the contemplative life becomes to others its condemnation. "They just sit there," it is said of enclosed religious, "you can see by their faces that they've never made an effort in their lives. And it's effort that counts." If there are lazy religious in contemplative houses—and there certainly are—they are neither the happy ones nor the ones to judge by. The serenity which comes from inertia and apathy can be distinguished at once from the serenity which comes of interior prayer. There is nothing sterile about interior prayer: it is wearing in the extreme. So secret is its intensity that, so far as measurable results go, the prayer of activity has the advantage every time. But if even human love can be deepest when undemonstrative, surely divine love need not be materialised when best expressed? Once admit that the energy of love as expressed in prayer is both secret and social—once, that is to say, you no longer demand statistics on the one hand or regard spirituality as being self-culture on the other—your case against contemplative orders falls to the ground. Not only does it fall to the ground but the reverse is proved true: interior prayer is apostolic, active, life-giving. No wonder St. Thomas ranks the contemplative vocation as the highest: in its perfection it supposes the perfection of the others. It includes, though bloodlessly, martyrdom.

THE WORLD'S MISSING LINK: CONTEMPLATION

We have seen that interior prayer begets—and, in its perfection, includes—the apostle's and even the martyr's vocation: greater love than this no man can have, than that he should lay down his life for his fellow men. Contemplation is the greater love, the better part. It is not only the most effective link between man and God but between man and man.

Leave out contemplation and what happens? Rejecting the opportunity of living on the highest supernatural plane, the soul has to manage as best it can with life lower down in the scale of grace. If it rejects prayer altogether, it lives according to nature and not according to grace at all. This means that the soul now suffers the whole range of restrictions from which contemplation could have liberated it. The spirit becomes as it were embedded in the flesh. This is not to say that the body is necessarily in control or that the intellect, as such, is impoverished. It is to say that the material elements which force themselves upon the senses and deflect the body from its perfection force themselves also upon the spirit and deflect it from *its* perfection. Such things as gratification of appetite, physical and mental suffering, outward circumstances connected with work and place and change and taste and health and time—contingencies of every kind—have power to influence a non-praying man in a way which would be impossible in the case of a man who contemplated. The reason why contemplatives remain undisturbed is not merely because they are detached—detachment is the effect rather than the cause—but that they are in a world of different values. This is not an imaginary world, it is the real one. The materialist and not the mystic is the artificial man: the true realist is the man who prays. The man who scorns prayer lives only on the surface of things: he never comes to see things as God sees them. Only the man who allows God to raise him from the natural to the supernatural can form any sort of idea of the inwardness of things. Contemplation does this. Grace does this. Nothing else does.

When the contemplative prays, then, he is operating on a plane which has no meaning for the materialist. He is doing something which is outside time, which does not register in space, which has no physical actuality. The materialist on the other hand, even when he prays, is far less free. Prayer, to him, is an uncertain quantity, an uncomfortable experiment, and he spends it in longing to get back to his own proper element with the dimensions which he knows. Whether in prayer or out of it he is always more or less open to delusion and disappointment and false judgement. He is at home only in the world of matter, and even here he makes many more mistakes than a contemplative would make in the same circumstances. Change and movement and concrete forms and unpredictable consequences make up the world which is familiar to the materialist. So, of course, his spiritual life is infected by these things. The natural has invaded the supernatural. Even the contemplative is not entirely free from the danger: physical experience and perceptions are always trying to leave their impression upon the spirit. It is only by directing the interior faculties more and more towards God that the material can be prevented from communicating itself to the spiritual.

The same, as before, goes for mankind as a whole. Leave out spirituality and the universe becomes a biological fact. Leave out relationship with God and the human race is a chance experiment subject to material improvement, material accident, material decline, material disruption. Where there is no supernatural destiny there can be no sureties.

Deny divine purpose to the world and human beings have every excuse for being worldly. Why not after all—if they are worldlings and no more?

Spirituality is not, then, one of those elements which we see in the world about us and which may or may not be taken up. The spiritual life has not been invented for the benefit of those who happen to have a taste for it. If it is what it says it is—namely a life—then it is part of human life as a whole. The world's life as well as the individual's. It is no good for people to admire the contemplative ideal at a distance and yet to deny the necessity of making even a beginning in prayer themselves. It is no good admitting that it is only the contemplative who is really clear about what he is aiming at if no attempt is made to aim at the same thing. If contemplatives alone are sure, then the remedy for the world's doubt is obvious. If it is only the contemplative who is properly poised, then only a contemplative mankind can realise its full perfection.

THE WORLD'S OTHER DEBT

From what has been said we find that prayer not only relates men to God but relates them also to one another. So if we take the spiritual link between mankind and God we see that it has a corporate quality. It is this social aspect of prayer which we are now to examine. The world's debt towards God is not only one of interior contemplation—social only in the sense of shared by all—but also one of public ceremonial worship.

Just as Christ gave Himself at the same time for the individual and the whole, so man gives himself individually and collectively back again to God. There is the personal, unique, incommunicable self who worships in a way evolved by the combination of his own effort and the Holy Spirit; there are the millions who must benefit by this exercise. Not only benefit but take part in it according to their own

personal, unique, and incommunicable manner. Though the
relationship may be spiritual, the association must be visible.
Each brings his incommunicable self to find communion in
the worship of the One. Not a mystical communion only,
but a corporate one. This is the prayer of Christ's visible
Church. This is the liturgy.

Now if God spoke to man through Christ, so man must
also speak to God through Christ. If the Father received
from His Son the perfect sacrifice of praise, then only in the
Person of the Son can man perfect his sacrifice to the Father.
This brings us to the climax of liturgical prayer, namely the
Mass. It is in the Mass that the Catholic is able to pay back
to God the debt which is owed to Him by all mankind.
Nothing but an infinitely perfect prayer could do this. The
Catholic knows that in the Mass Christ is taking the prayers
of each individual member of His mystical body, and in vir-
tue of what He, the Head, has merited, is giving to them a
value which is out of all proportion to their intensity. The
Catholic knows, moreover, that the collective needs of mankind are embraced in the Mass and presented to the Father.
Thus by uniting himself with the Priest and Victim the
Catholic is, during his Mass prayers, filling up what is wanting to the service owed by man. This is the Catholic's privilege—that he should help to extend the ministry of Christ.
As the sufferer is an extension of Christ suffering, as the
tempted is an extension of Christ struggling in the Garden
against the sins of man, so the soul who prays his Mass with
Christ is, whether he be layman or a priest, an extension of
Christ reclaiming souls from evil. *Pro vobis et pro multis
effundetur.* The *multis* means more than the multitude of
the devout.

As the Head of the body prays, so also do the limbs. In
the Mass is the complete answer to the necessity and insufficiency of man. Where men fail in their obligation and either
refuse to pay homage or else misinterpret the manner of its
expression, Christ, by sacrificing Himself, gives to those who
will look the pattern of praise.

Man, then, in belonging to the created human order belongs to a family. He is one of a true visible society. Each man is not an entity on his own but has responsibilities which are defined by the Creator of the order to which he belongs and expressed both individually and corporately. Having a body as well as a soul he must worship with his body as well as with his soul. If his whole life, physical and social as well as intellectual and supernatural, comes to him from God, then God must be recognised in every part of it. Not enough to worship from the mountainside and in the woods, communing privately with the Lord who made these things; there must be signs and ceremonies as well. How can there be a society if the members do not come to its meetings? Where is the family if the children are never seen? The language of the society is the liturgy, the bread of the family is the Body of Christ.

AND THEN COMES COMMUNISM

As a subject Communism has become the darling chestnut of the Catholic press. Rightly has much space been devoted to it: it touches the faithful at every point. Yet surprisingly little is known about it by the average Catholic who has come to take it for granted and regards the whole thing as either a bore or an intellectual challenge which is beyond him. "Oh, *that* again," I heard a young man exclaim today when his attendance at a lecture on Communism was being canvassed, "but we've heard it all before, and it doesn't affect this country anyway. Our sort of Communist isn't the Soviet kind . . . he's merely the old-fashioned Radical under a new name." This attitude of mind is sufficiently general to warrant a brief survey of what Communism stands for and what weapons Catholicism possesses to combat it.

We do not need to know much of the Marxist theory to see that it is the antithesis of what we have been advocating in the last three sections. "Worship of any sort, whether contemplative or liturgical", says the Communist, "is a denial of the temporal end of man. The religious idea is a fabrication designed to cover the failure of man to find human happiness in the material world." For the Communist there is only one reality; to him existence means physical existence in a world of sense; in his scheme the values on which traditional civilisation has been founded are meaningless; the material is the beginning and end of everything.

In claiming that the temporal well-being of mankind is the absolute, Communism pledges itself automatically to a warfare against the Church. Notice that it is the well-being of *society* which is pointed to as the ultimate goal, and not the well-being of those who make up society. On this head too, therefore, the Christian ideal with its emphasis on individual rights is an obstacle to be eliminated. Where the Church preaches the dignity of each separate created soul, Communism preaches the sanctity of the collective. Each man is the property of the Party; the Party has no respect for human personality. Personal integrity has neither meaning nor value to Communism except in so far as it serves the programme. The only morality recognised by Communism is that which is defined by the needs of world revolution: you are good or bad entirely according to how far you are or are not in line with the Party conscience.[1] The Party conscience may express itself differently in different countries, meeting particular resistances according to the interpretation put upon local situations by the Kremlin, but the general drift is clear enough. The promptings of the Communist conscience are guided solely by the ambitions of the proletariat.

So stated, the Communist idea would seem to be almost too impersonal and dictatorial to be in the least attractive to the minds of men. Wherein, then, lies its appeal? How account for its remarkable growth? It is matter for shame to us Christians that what people like about Communism is

[1] "Whatsoever is useful to the Communist Party is moral, and whatsoever is unfavourable to it is immoral." *Party Ethics*, which is a standard Communist text-book drawn up by Jaroslavsky, the leader of the Militant Atheists.

precisely what they should be liking about Christianity—if
the Christians only revealed it more. The neophyte sees in
Communism the sacrifices which its members are prepared
to make for the sake of the whole, he sees the social conscience at work in numberless reforms, he sees a genuine
enthusiasm for an ideal, he sees the cause of the poor taken
up against exploitation by the rich, he sees—particularly if he
has not come across religion—an answer to his inner yearnings
for something noble to which he can dedicate his life. He
makes a mysticism of the Marxist theory. He wants to give
glory to the collective and to walk in the way of its saints.

The moment we examine this Marxist theory we see at
once that if you are willing to leave out the grace of God
and a supernatural purpose you will find a good enough
cause to champion. If you take, as Karl Marx took, the realisation of human perfection as being achieved with the
establishment of a classless society, then your own personal
perfection is measured by the altruism of your effort. Your
activity reaches its highest peak when you are sublimating
yourself in the interests of society at large. Thus if your aim
is the "people's" happiness, and if in the attempt to effect it
you are to find your own happiness as well, you commit
yourself, as things are in the world, to revolution. The Communist is accordingly a missioner or he is nothing; he has a
revelation, he preaches a gospel. Because he is prepared to
be a martyr he is ready to be a persecutor. He is so convinced
of the truth which he holds that anyone who holds to another
truth must be eliminated. The sincere Communist is just as
high-minded about it all as we are about Catholicism. His
methods are different but the principle is the same.

We, as Catholics and belonging to a different civilisation,
have no doubt that Communism leads to evil. This should
not blind us to the fact that the rank and file of Communists
are honestly wanting a good. If we can forget for the moment the Cominform and remember the soul of the individual Communist we are far more likely to help the cause of
Christianity. To do this is to reverse the totalitarian ideology,
and so cannot fail to be a move in the right direction. In our

claim that every man, of whatever station in life, has an inalienable selfhood, a power of determining the course he is to take, and that this is what he inherits as a free-born son of God, we can hardly be said to favour the capitalist at the expense of the working man. A man is master of his own life and soul even if he is master of nothing else. "No," says Communism, "he is master of nothing. He is the property of the whole." Our fight is not so much *against* Communism as *for* the soul of the Communist. If we have any sort of real love for souls, praying for them and working for them, we shall be turning upon them the only force which is powerful enough to detach them from their Satanic movement. The grace of God does not as a rule dawn unless something more than a direct hit has been scored. Even if the Church militant were as combative as militant Communism it is doubtful whether much could be done. But if the members of the Church militant were more spiritual than their opposite numbers are material it would be a different question altogether. We should then have nothing to fear from our enemies.

CRUSADE OR CAPITULATION

Having seen briefly what Communism stands for, we turn now to the means by which it may be met. If it is the aim of Communism to transform society by developing it in one direction it is the aim of the Church to transform it by development in the other. If the new imperialism hopes to establish itself by means of anarchy then it is by restoration and not by revolution that Christianity must meet it. So if there is to be a return to Christian principles, one thing is absolutely necessary—the faithful must know what they are.

It is surprising how few Catholics recognise the duty of studying the doctrines and social programmes of the Church. It is probably true to say that the first reason why Communism has gained such ground—gained it so rapidly and held it so firmly—is that the ordinary Communist knows exactly what he wants whereas the ordinary Christian does not. This is far from claiming that every Soviet worker has an expert understanding of the Party's objectives while every Catholic takes his catechism for granted; it is simply to claim that the U.S.S.R. demands more in the way of practical and intellectual allegiance—and sees that it gets it. At Communist headquarters it is estimated that ten thousand members leave the Party every year for no other reason than that they cannot keep up with their party obligations. These ex-members are not apostates. They believe; they look forward to the realisation of the Marxist dream. It is merely that they are not judged to be equipped with what is demanded by their creed. A system which has no regard for the individual soul can afford to work along these lines. The Church cannot say "Get up your theology or get out". Communism can, and does, say "Study your Karl Marx, preach it, give your time to it, and if we of the Party happen to want your children or your wife you must be ready to hand over". If the would-be member is unable to accept these terms he is no use, and out he goes. This twofold obligation which rests upon every Communist, the duty of knowing the theory and of being willing to sacrifice to it in practice, is kept in a studiously even ratio of fifty-fifty. The Party member may not excuse himself from the work of active propagation on the grounds that he is the brains of the movement; nor may the agitator or distributor cut down his study of Marxist principle and history. If total revolution—in social, moral, political, economic and international spheres—is required, so also is total service. The pace of every movement has been quickened more effectively by sacrifice than by any other force. Both Communism and Christianity believe in blood.

Our first necessity, then, is to know as much about religion as the Communist knows about revolution. We have revelation, tradition, dogma, the Church's social theory to draw from; he has Engels and Marx (with his *Capital* and *Communist Manifesto*). Where we have the Fathers, the Doctors of the Church, the Schoolmen, the more recent Popes with their Encyclicals, and a vast corpus of up-to-date literature on property, the family, and social justice—apart altogether from the specifically spiritual writings of the Church which assume, even where they do not positively preach, the same principles—Communists have their counterpart in the resolutions passed from time to time by the Party, in the works of Lenin, in Stalin's explanations of the Communist gospel, in Jaroslavsky's *Party Ethics*, in Dimitrov's policy of underground recruitment and Thorez's plan for gradual infiltration. The only difference in the approach to the opposing body of authorities is that whereas we leave it to the experts, our enemies demand it of the rank and file.

The practical implications of all this are obvious. They may take various forms, but if we are to resist Communism they must take some form. We must be ready to take measures which, if not heroic in their response to the call of sacrifice, are at least likely to be exceedingly boring in prospect. We may have to attend lectures, read up the encyclicals, enter discussions, find out what is the Church's attitude towards education, marriage problems, wages, strikes, and so on. The Catholic, no less than the Communist, never finally graduates: he goes on learning his faith. The trouble is that when it comes to the point of defending that faith, the Communist jumps onto the platform with his mind full of facts, debating gambits, figures and oratorical fireworks; and the Catholic runs a mile. Every time the Catholic runs his mile, the Communist both points the finger of scorn and makes use of the empty place. The score is registered, the Church suffers a defeat.

Thus if the conflict between Communism and Christianity is primarily one of principle before even it is one of practice, it is clearly up to the Christian to have the mind of Christ before he can even begin to act with the acts of Christ. If Lenin came down like a ton of bricks on those who thought that by liquidating their opponents they could somehow bypass the doctrine of dialectic materialism, then surely in the same way we may insist that the only preparation for the converting of our rivals in the field—let alone for the launching of any sort of effective Christian propaganda—is instruction. Nothing, heaven knows, could be more sacrificial. Of all the forms of Christian *ascesis,* receiving instruction is perhaps the most irksome. It can only be equalled by the *ascesis* of actually giving it. Not only fearless and enthusiastic must be the statement of our faith, not only pungent must be the exposition of our policy, not only idealistic must be our spirituality in its drive against the false doctrine of materialism—but reasoned and realistic must all this be as well.

THE POSSIBLE REMEDY

How, in view of what we have been considering, can we help taking a dismal view of the future? For a moment let us restate the case against us, and then review the potential which is on our side. In fact the rest of this book will be mostly about the potential which is on our side. It is our purpose to make that potential actual—and to keep it going at full strength for as long as life is left to us. We sing while there's voice to sing with. Neither pronouncements from the Kremlin nor the rumblings of Russian guns have power to silence the song of contemplation. This particular voice comes from the heart of the Church, and the gates of hell shall not prevail against it.

Seeing then all round us the forces of evil—active, fanatical, efficient, spreading with a rapidity which challenges our own mark of catholicity in its best periods—and seeing at the same time among the faithful a dangerous apathy, a hideous ignorance of the menace which threatens us, an almost superstitious trust in some sort of providential immunity, we begin to wonder how on earth the Church can survive the present emergency. In a sense our very virtues as Christians are, in crises of this sort, the qualities which take the bite out of whatever opposition we are able to rouse. Our readiness to forgive, our love of peace, our regard for the individual soul are attitudes which disarm us almost before we have begun to mobilise. Ever so slightly misunderstood, or influenced at all by laziness, our imagined Christian acceptance and faith can become something perilously near to Eastern fatalism. Our sense of ultimate victory, the confidence of knowing that the Church must survive, the habit of living in terms of centuries rather than in terms of decades or general strikes or persecutions or financial depressions are apt to have an enervating effect so far as material effort is concerned. Even the knowledge that we ourselves, individuals, are cared for by a loving God who will not let us perish, and that whatever may go wrong in our lives we have an eternity of happiness to look forward to, can be conducive to an irresponsibility which is bad. The Communist, on the other hand, has no such chance of misreading his charter. For him the mission is immediate and clear. There are no long-term views in his case: if he does not get what he wants in this life he has nothing else to look forward to. His atheism acts as a spur. There is a pressing urgency about everything he undertakes; each new opening may bring in the revolution, every crack in the defences of the old order, of Christianity, must be widened.

For instance. When we pray for the conversion of Russia do we really imagine that it will come about in our time? When we ask to be defended in the day of battle do we include in this idea the possibility of really having to fight for our faith? The Communist mentality, being wholly materialist, is entirely different. The training is for frontline warfare. Shock tactics, secret manœuvres, sudden changes of front are part of the general preparation. The Communist drill-book is nothing if not opportunist. Possessing no morality, no absolute standards save those dictated by the need of the Party at the moment, Communist policy may alter abruptly from day to day. Not only policy but doctrine may be altered by the Kremlin at a moment's notice to suit the requirements of Soviet propaganda in a particular country, to secure a majority vote, to suppress disaffection within its own ranks. With us truth is fixed, with them not. With them nothing may stand in the way of material advantage. This is logical enough since they believe in no other.

Now if material advantages for the many—in other words social conditions—are the whole concern of the Communist

ideology, then it is the business of Catholicism to provide a
working alternative to the Communist solution. That is to say
if bad social conditions are the appropriate medium of dia-
lectical materialism and if good ones are its professed aim,
then these two extremes of the same problem must be investi-
gated by the Church and a social system be evolved. At this
stage the Church can turn round on us and say "Ah, but I've
had one for generations. The truth is that none of you will
take the trouble to study it."

The Church does not exist solely to teach people dogmatic
theology. The properly instructed Catholic should be able to
show that a real relationship exists between dogma and morality, between the theory of the faith and the living problems of society. Catholics are inclined to be too departmental
about their religion, concentrating almost exclusively upon
that department of it which has to do with personal sanctification. There should be a balance between theoretical, spiritual, and practical religion. Indeed there should not merely
be a balance but an interaction: each is an aspect of the same
thing. If the material conditions of mankind were meant to be
outside the scope of the individual man's conscience the
Church would not have bothered to frame a social policy.
But this is just what the Church, particularly through its
recent succession of Popes, has done. There exists a body of
social teaching just as there exists a body of dogmatic and
moral teaching. But the faithful, taken by and large, are not
conversant with it. The faithful resent instruction in these
matters; the clergy are shy of labouring its necessity. Just as
laziness and false humility are responsible for the almost complete ignorance of mystical theology among the majority of
Catholics, lay and clerical alike, so laziness and the equally
false sense of minding one's own business are responsible for
ignorance regarding the Church's social teaching. "The whole
thing is too political, and it would be better if the Church
kept out of it . . . perhaps it's all propaganda . . . if the
Church *has* to mix itself up with the affairs of the State, then
it's a thing for the hierarchy and not for us . . . let the Ro-

man Curia take the responsibility. . . ." The opportunity is missed and the ignorance goes on.

Any system which promises to remedy the social injustice in the world is bound to be listened to, and if the followers of religion are silent the only alternative for the enquirer is to join the followers of revolution. If Catholics lived as fully functioning Catholics, and if Christian states accepted the implications of Christianity, there would be no case for revolution. It is only because the Church's social code has never been lived that there has come to be anything to rebel against.

The possession of the requisite knowledge and the willingness to communicate it are, then, the only obstacle which is likely to stand in the way of Communist domination. For us it means the Cross. It means a Crusade. If the hammer and sickle are not suffered to remain idle and collect the rust, nor may the Cross and the Crown of Thorns be kept in the background for purposes of private devotion. Where the Soviet emblems point downwards, beating flat and cutting away at the roots, the emblems of Christianity point upwards to the skies, inviting to compassion and coronation. Communism aims at hammering the world into shape; Christianity aims at re-shaping it according to the Gospel. Where the Communist discards both natural rights and morals in his search for rational materialism, the Christian sees in liberty and morality the return to reason. There has never in man's history been a campaign towards personal and political integrity without the Cross. The question is now whether a part of that Cross is not going to involve a period of suppression and underground struggle. That the Church will survive is not, as we have seen, a matter of doubt. But it seems on the face of it quite probable that it will have to fight for its very existence.

THE POSSIBLE ECLIPSE

With the failure to present our alternative to Communism— at all events in such a form as will be found sufficiently acceptable to the non-Communist world—we are in grave danger of being left behind in the competition for world evangelisation. This is not to lay the blame on any one department of the Church; it is simply to state an unpleasantly evident fact. It is further to suggest that the omission may well, at least in the outward struggle, be followed by a loss of ground and even, possibly, by a temporary eclipse. Now though it may be necessary to the development of the Church that we should suffer such a reverse—the mystical body of the Church subjected to the kind of mystical dark night which is endured by the soul in contemplation—it would surely be the greatest mistake to act on this assumption and passively let things take their course. God's plan *may* involve a suspension of the Church's spread in Western Europe—and in Eastern Europe, Asia, Africa, and the Americas as well if it comes to that—but it is surely fatal to expect it. "What has happened before in history can happen again now" is a dispirited approach; it should be indulged only with reference to the opposite outcome. The idea of necessary purification, the idea that the race has sinned and must take its punishment, is true enough up to a point. But it is a doctrine which can be misinterpreted.[1] If the emphasis is upon the punishment rather than upon the sin it is difficult to see where the element of true penance comes in. First recognise the guilt and then begin to talk about expiation. Nations as well as individuals have a way of talking a lot about expiation in the hopes that it will not be noticed how much they cling to the sin.

It is always easier to shrug one's shoulders, particularly if one is a collective body with national or racial shoulders, and say, "Now we are in for a dark age, a night of blackout for civilisation, so there is nothing to do but go to sleep and wait for the dawn." If culture and the outward forms of religion are to be swept away by the new savagery of Communism it may or may not be a punishment—and we certainly have de-

[1] As, for instance, it was misinterpreted by Marshal Pétain in connection with the Nazi occupation of France. If the means of averting disaster are neglected the attitude is no better than one of supine fatalism.

served punishment of some sort—but it does not mean that we have to let go of culture and the outward forms of religion. If the Western tradition *does* go down under the dark pressure of materialism it is only our refusal to acquiesce that will enable it to revive again.

As individuals we may have little enough chance of influencing the policy to be pursued against Communism, but as individuals we shall have the greatest possible chance of keeping that policy going. The Church does not depend upon its policies, but upon the fidelity of its members. The rock of faith on which the Church rests—the rock which is Christ and His successors—is more surely found in the faithful than in systems of foreign relations. It will be by the existence of personal fidelity to the light, pin-points gleaming in the blackness of unbelief, that the return of an eclipsed faith is guaranteed. It was when in turn Egypt, Assyria, Chaldea, Persia, Greece and Rome thought Israel to be finished that Israelites, scattered and with no outward observance to point to, were preserving in their own lives the heritage of their fathers, awaiting the day of their deliverance. In the same way it was when Europe was dominated by the Franks, by the Goths, by the Huns, by the Vandals, that Christianity was judged to have collapsed along with the Latin culture which had enshrined it. In fact, of course, neither Christianity nor its traditional culture had gone down before the successive invasions of barbarism: they had merely gone, for a time, underground. Just as the Old Testament Jews stood by the Lord, and the New Testament Christians stood by Christ, so with us if the test comes along: our safety lies in standing, in clinging, in believing. Our faith—by which we mean our hope and charity as well—is the rock on which Communism will break. We are the Church, and the Church is Christ. Christ pledges Himself to His members, entrusts Himself to His members, depends upon the fidelity of His members.

If the world, then, is to be preserved from universal anarchy and universal hate, it must return, consciously and by professed choice, to Christ. Nothing but our Christian way of life, our moral principles and specifically Christian institutions and interpretations, can save mankind. Christianity and Communism are mutually exclusive.[2] Neither is *a* way of life, *an* alternative to choose from out of many. Each is an absolute. The two radical ideas are in complete opposition. There can be no gradual retreat—each, without loss of face, condoning the other. It is Christ or anti-Christ, and it is for the world to choose. The world must choose Christ or perish. Not now any more an issue for the European world to resolve for its own social and international convenience, but for the whole world. This Gospel must be preached to all mankind. If our Gospel is not so preached, the other will be. And then?

PAIN AS A FOURTH DIMENSION

The whole animal kingdom is subject to suffering. To the kingdom of the rational animal alone is given the power to suffer willingly—even happily. Only man is able to transmute pain, and it is a prerogative which can, all too easily, be overlooked. If suffering is offered to the lord of creation for what he can make of it, then the more clearly it is seen in relation

---

[2] "The masses cannot be really happy until they have been deprived of illusory happiness by the abolition of religion" is one of Marx's primary postulates. Lenin is no less explicit: "Our programme necessarily includes the propaganda of atheism . . . the Marxist must be the enemy of religion." Lastly Stalin: "If you believe in God you render yourself guilty of treason against the revolution." If these opinions have been modified to the extent of permitting a state-controlled Church in Russia it is only a manœuvre intended to suggest good will, it cannot signify recognition of spiritual claims. Communism may not make concessions of any real meaning to what is directly contrary to its essential purpose. "Our aim is not to 'renovate' the Church," states *Working Moscow,* "but to abolish it, to eradicate all religion." Article 122 of the Soviet Criminal Code runs as follows: "Teaching children or minors the principles of religious faith will be punished by correctional compulsory labour." This was re-issued in 1945.

to the purpose both of the world and of the individual soul the better.

The world is always, at every stage in its development, in labour. Nothing comes to the birth save by pain. If in the present phase of history we see more of the anguish than we do of the birth this should not blind us to the fact that grief and struggle can be the compelling force which liberates truth and virtue. Pain may be, under grace, the only possible means of effecting the liberation. It may be the only quality strong enough, acting like a blow-lamp, to burn away the layers of artificiality and materialism with which the world has been veneered by civilisation. But if the process is to work effectively it must, as we have seen in an earlier chapter, be taken up in the spirit of penance. Austerity may be forced upon the world by economic conditions, but unless it is received as the price to be paid for being able to occupy the place in God's plan which He wants it to occupy it is to a certain extent wasted. Its *main* function is missed. But whether pain is invited by God as an acknowledged penance or exacted by Him from an unwilling creation as an accumulated debt, it inevitably represents a chance: it forces an issue, it parts the ways, it outlines a possible solution to the mystery of life.

In the very act of paying the debt of his sins—so far as God allows him to in this world—a man may discover a new dimension. He can arrive, if he takes the trouble to follow up the light which the challenge of suffering gives rise to in his soul, at a new understanding of the world. He is given the chance of seeing creation as a pattern and in perspective. He can draw upon a new form of expression. For the non-Christian, suffering can be the means of learning the significance of Christ's life; for the Christian it is one of the means of sharing it and spreading it. "As we have been closely fitted into the pattern of His death," says St. Paul to the Romans, "so we have to be closely fitted into the pattern of His resurrection." In being fitted into the pattern of Christ's Passion the soul comes to a more subtle and intense perception, the mind comes to a new comprehension.

The mental adjustment of finding new focus in suffering

should not be any great difficulty for those who have the Gospel before them. There is the witness of the saints who bear out the same principle, there is the traditional doctrine of voluntary purification and vicarious atonement for sin. The question for us who live more or less in the acceptance of all this is how to convince the non-Christian that pain does not impoverish human nature but enriches it: it is the essentially Christian paradox of dying in order to live. How, except by suffering in a Christian way ourselves, can we possibly get across to the materialist the spiritualising value of pain? He will not take it on faith because he has not got any. Nor will he—and you can hardly expect him to—experiment in the doctrine himself. So it remains for us to prove to him that pain sharpens and refines, that voluntary renunciation actually humanises, that familiarity with grief and loneliness and near-despair is a uniting force between man and man.

If the Passion of Christ places us on a different level of merit from the natural level which would otherwise be ours it gives us also a different channel of expression—almost an added faculty. Our sufferings come to speak to God and to our own fellow sufferers in a language which is specifically Christ's. Though belonging to the physical order we have, through prayer and suffering, a claim upon another order altogether. What our baptism entitles us to by the merits of Christ becomes, through prayer and suffering, the familiar element of our lives. Now if there is this relationship between man and God, between the physical world and the spiritual, it follows that those who exercise their faculties of spiritual expression are, to a much greater extent than those who do not, responsible for the progress and support of the world. It is almost as if God entrusts His interests to the men of prayer and the men of suffering instead of to the men of affairs and the men of consequence.[1] The real weight rests on the Church praying and the Church penitent.

Dom Louis Merton (Thomas Merton who wrote *Elected*

---

[1] "God has chosen what the world holds base and contemptible, what the world holds weak, so as to condemn the strong." I Corinthians i, 27.

Silence) wonders "if there are twenty men alive in the world now who see things as they really are." It would mean, he says, finding twenty whose hearts and minds were free, who had attached themselves to neither spiritual graces nor created things. "I don't believe that there are twenty such men in the world. But there must be one or two. They are the ones who are holding everything together and keeping the universe from falling apart."[2] This is a claim which cannot be proved, but each of us knows that it must be true. What Father Louis attributes to detachment is here attributed to the combined influence of prayer and suffering. They amount in the end to the same thing. Prayer, detachment, suffering for God's sake—whatever you like to call it that gives to a soul the vision of the universe as it really is—must inevitably amount to the most powerful force in the world. This is what we have meant by finding a fourth dimension. Rooted in substance we realise not only our final end but also our present operation—in spirit.

THE PATTERN OF THE SPIRIT

We have seen that man belongs to both worlds, the material and the spiritual. But though he has the entry into both, he has to be pushed into one of them. He is on really familiar ground only in the world of the senses; for the other he has to shut his eyes and make acts of faith. It is only later on, when he has learned more about it, that he can open his eyes wide and, by looking at the world about him, learn even more about the two orders to which he belongs. By nature man apprehends only natural reality—which is a very small part of reality indeed. By grace he begins to apprehend reality at another level altogether. When prayer has been preached to him and when suffering has been exhibited to him for what it really is—though, of course, he may come to the knowledge of the value of suffering by experiencing it himself—and above

[2] *Seeds of Contemplation*, p. 124.

all when the light of grace has lit up his intelligence so that he can see beyond the rim of physical perception, he is able to give and receive—in relation both to God and to man—in his two appropriate worlds at the same time. Now this is not a take-it-or-leave-it activity, a please-yourself expression. It is an essential part of man's equipment in his progress towards God.

Because man cannot detach himself from his essential purpose his soul is perpetually in search for a solution which will resolve the difficulty of living in two worlds at once. Anyone who has ever thought at all and who is not a complete fool must be aware of the fact that one of the first necessities which he is up against in this life is that of combining the material and spiritual elements of the world in which he lives and making of them a harmony. He achieves this object not by separating the two elements and concentrating upon each in turn, but by uniting them and being true to each. In his capacity as natural-plus-supernatural being he is intended by God to bring about such a fusion. The grace is there. He can do it. The saints are those who have managed it best; everyone else manages more or less—according to how far the saints' purpose is kept in view.

It is true that all except perhaps the greatest saints and mystics—and possibly even these for a good deal of the time —are conscious of one element more keenly than of the other, but even though their senses tell them more of matter than grace seems to tell them of spirit they at least know that their souls go infinitely beyond whatever their senses are able to assimilate. They know too that this spiritual operation is vastly more important to them than any other. Indeed for those who have advanced any distance in the way of the mystics, but who have not yet got settled in it, the danger is to imagine that the spiritual world is the only one that matters and that they need not concern themselves with perfecting their existence in the physical one. The effort to live the supernatural life in its perfection has a way of making the soul impatient of the natural. It can't escape the natural, but it would like to. It feels the pressure of the material world more than it feels the compensating pressure of the spiritual world. It wants to have but one world to worry about. The desire which begins with repudiating self may end by repudiating nature. But it is only the fallen side of nature which must be repudiated: repudiate the whole of it and you get inhumanity. Both worlds have to be lived in—since both are God's. Where the hedonist throws out the balance by living in the world of sense and refusing to concern himself with any other, the too ardent would-be mystic throws it out by trampling on finite creation.

Such a tendency on the part of the incompletely developed soul of prayer is understandable enough. To one who has even begun to appreciate the pattern of reality, the utter disparity which is seen in the created world appears at once fantastic and tragic. Human affairs seem as mad as *Iolanthe* but not as harmless. To the novice in contemplation everything is not only upside down but pointing Satanwards. So of course to him the only way out is to have as little to do as possible with whatever has no direct relation to God. The outcome of this is that the quality of understanding is obscured, and sympathy inevitably suffers. It means that a human soul is trying to sever its connection with its own roots. It is forgetting its own humanity. It is making a big mistake.

The remedy against approaching life in this way is not what would at first appear as being the most obvious. It is not to cut down prayer and thus get a more balanced view of creatures. It is on the contrary to develop and extend prayer, and thus get a more Godlike view of them. The more the soul praises God, the more it sees, without necessarily noticing the difference of focus, the inwardness of creatures. Contemplation is the influence above all others which heightens the soul's perceptions. From seeing only the surface, the soul comes by means of its prayer to appreciate significances. Contemplation gives us the setting. The concrete world is smaller than the spiritual, and can be properly understood only in its setting—which is up against the larger world of the spirit. To see either by itself is to see it incompletely. Contemplation not only opens the inward eye but puts foreground and background in their right perspectives.

THE SHAPE OF THE PRESENT PURPOSE

We have seen that the created order is real enough but that it does not stand in its own right. It needs a further reference. It needs to be looked at with the truly realist eye of the contemplative. Where the expert, the technician, the experimental scientist can give us the *what* of an object, the man of interior vision can give us the *whence* and the *why*. The soul of prayer goes beyond composition to what is much more important—namely *being*. If you get meaning, motive and essence—over and above what the experts can tell you about the substance—you get pretty well as much of a thing as you are likely to want.

Apply all this to the responsibility of the present moment as seen in the light of the ultimate responsibility. The contemplative, with his realist and more or less constant awareness of eternity, is able, as others are not, to appreciate the enormous possibilities of the present moment. The implications may be alarming to him, but at least they are *there*—and they are true. The present moment does, as a fact, derive its significance from its setting in the whole. It has the same uniqueness as each of the single creations in the physical order, it has the same potential sacredness, the same chances of being wasted or misused. As with creatures, so with moments: the contemplative knows what has led up to them, can trace the continuity in the scheme. Past, present, and future are so related as to form a unity—a unity which finds its focus-point in the shifting now. Not that the soul always feels the comfort of enjoying this unity—on the contrary it is usually the contemplative who, more than other people, has to make acts of faith about the providential ordering of his life—but at least there is the admission in the will that everything, however unintelligible from the human point of view, is, if taken in relation to God's all-comprehensive plan, of a piece. Indeed *however* chaotic the existing situation, it can be accepted as the expression of God's permissive will. The existing situation may be the outcome of mixed motives, may be caused by innumerable mistakes, may crown a process of malice and deceit, but the point is that *here and now* there is a moment which exactly represents the will of God. His will is identified with the present need. Whatever deviations went before, there is a perfect fit at last.

The contemplative realises as nobody else does that each separate minute is not only a climax of past happenings, an arrival platform after round-about travel, but that it is also the beginning of future ones, a departure platform for a journey which goes on into eternity. Each new moment is a junction. There are no real stops; changes at all the stations are the condition of this particular progress; every change allowed for—indeed having its destined place—in the plan of God. The haphazard does not enter in—any more than does the idea of fatalism.

"I can think of nothing *more* fatalistic", might be an objection, "than to conceive of a scheme which provides such a necessary relationship between cause and effect." The answer is surely that the contemplative, in seeing how closely cause and effect interact with regard to past and future, sees also how closely grace and freewill interact with regard to the immediate present. The very powers which lead the interior soul to an appreciation of the responsibility of the passing moment lead him away from the danger of determinism. His faith, more sensitive and more widely applied, rescues him from fatalism. To a soul who is settled in God the idea that untold quantities of influences have gone to make up a certain circumstance, that factors outside personal control altogether are being brought to bear, that possibilities are being opened up which cannot be imagined, is not a cramping thought. Quite the reverse. It is a stimulant. The influences are not untold to God. If the factors are outside the control of man there is all the more reason to see them as being under the control of God. The fact that the future is hidden to human intelligence makes it all the more necessary to hand over the whole thing to the care of Wisdom itself. You may say that this is not the way in which most people's minds can be made to work. Perhaps not. But whose fault is this? If most people contemplated there would be no difficulty. If most people contemplated there would be recognition of the truth. And it happens to be true that God rules His universe while man is allowed to help Him in the work. This is no novel discovery, it is a primary truth accepted by all who believe. It is a doctrine which finds its point of focus on what we have called the present moment's shape and purpose. Like all doctrines, it expands in the life of faith. It becomes almost limitless to those who contemplate. Time is felt to have form. And in practice the incidental is sacramentalised, canalised, revalued.

Thus if not everyone can be expected to make use of the above principles, at least it must be admitted that the above principles are true. At least it must be admitted that the soul of prayer, far from living in a dream world, faces facts. It is the so-called practical man, the active soul who gets through his day as the hedonist gets through his pleasures, who is the loser. He sees only a slice of time; the contemplative sees the whole as well as the slice—and sees both of them more clearly. Time, to the active soul, is something which comes out of a clock: it is measured by degrees. He can never really make terms with time because he mistakes its limits for its reality. The contemplative on the other hand, because his mind is set towards eternity, understands the principle of time. He is intimate, as others cannot be, with real time.

THE FINAL SYNTHESIS

There is an Arab proverb to the effect that the pomegranate is not the pips and the pips are not the pomegranate, but that one is all and all are one. It probably sounds better in Arabic. In order to grasp what the world as a whole is all about, and at the same time to appreciate the relations which exist both between the creatures which compose it and between them and God, we need to go about it with a positive theory and not merely to content ourselves by saying what the world's purpose and nature are not. We cannot afford, that is to say, to take no interest in material creation on the grounds that our whole concern is with the supernatural. "The invisible things are clearly seen," St. Paul reminds the Romans, "being understood by the things that are made." If we turn our backs on the things that are made we are in the paradoxical position of tripping up on the things that are unmade. If we paid no attention to creatures we would be dividing the principle of charity. Neither God nor love nor happiness nor creation, natural and supernatural, may be divided against themselves. The apparently conflicting claims are fulfilled not by denying the one and concentrating on the other, but by getting perfectly clear the nature of each and getting the best out of both. Positive, therefore, not negative. We find, we do not abstract. Abstraction may be necessary when trying to arrive at the nature of God, but it does not help a great deal when trying to arrive at an understanding of life. Happiness is more than not-misery, love more than not-hate, prayer more than not-distraction, work more than not-sloth. What we must look for in each case is the actuality: what the thing is and what it points to. We must see it in relation to the over-all. The pips in the pomegranate: the pomegranate in the pips.

How do we come by this sort of vision? It is, again, part of the mental habit induced by the practice of serious interior prayer. The soul of prayer assimilates truth as the beings assimilate air. The process is unplanned. It simply happens. Take, for instance, the exercise of prayer as practised by the contemplative soul. There is a certain necessary negation at first—the soul excludes as far as it can the alien elements—but as soon as the mind has detached itself from the love and the memory of creatures it heads positively towards God. It is the hindering love of creatures which is renounced, not the lovable nature of creatures. Creatures are respected: the *being* of the creature is known to be good: the perfections of the creature are swept up in the general reference to God.

Only when the creature has been spoiled by misuse is it

treated with severity by the saint. Saints are sometimes hard on wealth, and quite particularly hard on wine and other luxuries, but they are much harder upon themselves for loving these things inordinately. Rightly used, they would not be objected to by the saints. As soon as the saint can assure himself that he no longer wants creatures for their own sake or for his own he becomes surprisingly mild about them. He says what nice things they are. Which is true. They were made good by God—as He Himself was the first to record. When the soul, by means of the ascetic and mystical life, has arrived at the stage of handling creatures without hurt he can see how good they are. And seeing how good they are, he can begin to teach others how to handle them without hurt. But he must be careful, because there can be a lot of humbug about all this.

Few things show up the difference between the bogus and the true in matters of the spirit as clearly as this question of the approach to creatures and created pleasure. To the false mystic and ascetic creatures are either entirely despicable or, by contrast, too freely indulged in; to the genuine they are respected, kept somewhat at arms' length, given thanks for when necessity has provided their enjoyment. The former creates a gulf between God and His works, the latter achieves a synthesis. Like Moses seeing from the summit of Phasga the land of Canaan stretched out before him, the contemplative sees the created order with its hills and hollows, with its movement and light, with its song and silence, rolling away towards the horizon. He sees the thing as a whole, and has no need to divide the landscape from—if there is such a word—the skyscape. To him the two are merged in the mists at the limit of his vision.

"All men are vain in whom there is not the knowledge of God," says the author of *Wisdom* in the thirteenth chapter, "and who by these good things that are seen could not understand Him that is. Neither by attending to the works have they acknowledged who was the workman . . . for by the greatness of the beauty of the creature, the Creator may be seen." If Solomon wrote these words, then he, if anyone did, needed to remind himself of their import. But the traps which were open for Solomon are those which are liable to catch any of us. We can be safe from them only if we pray. Prayer alone lifts the soul to the level where the works of God's hands are seen as the reflexions of God's Beauty. The believer can give a notional assent—and then go away and forget about it. To the contemplative the doctrine is experienced—and carried about with him as a habit.

THE SONG OF THE LITURGY

If there has to be a synthesis in seeing visually and spiritually, there has also to be a synthesis in praying vocally and mentally. Just as it would be a form of snobbishness to pretend an exclusive attention to the things of the spirit, so it would be a form of snobbishness to look down on the use of words in prayer. The abstract painter cannot boast that he has pursued his abstractions so far as to have no further use for colour or canvas or created forms. The higher mathematician does not despise the multiplication table: he is drawing upon it all day long. The brain specialist takes into consideration and even treats with respect, though he may not be able to cure, the common headache. By the same token the contemplative cannot think it beneath him to take part in liturgical worship. The liturgy is to his prayer what the notes are to music. The contemplative does not wait till the psalms are over before he can get down to the real business of prayer. What he does is to pray them contemplatively. The Divine Office is not to him a separate and somewhat inferior exercise, it is a continuation of the same interior exercise but expressed in a different form.

If it can be established that liturgical prayer has a contemplative significance then the charge which is most often brought against repeated recitation of both Offices and devotions falls to the ground. Once grant that the primary function of public worship is not the performance but the praise, it follows that prayerfulness is more important than ceremonial. Neither the rubrics nor the various forms of chant are ends in themselves, and where they fail to promote prayerfulness they are liable to get in the way of it. The liturgy is a song only when it is in tune with the worshipping mind and heart. Otherwise it is a noise. Words, melodies, gestures—in fact all outward expressions of devotion—are necessary to us because we are flesh and blood. Being body as well as spirit we cannot praise properly without these things. But they are a concession all the same. They are invented to make things easier for *us* in the relationship of prayer: they are not there to make things easier for God. He is praised by the attitude of heart, and if the attitude of heart is lacking there is no value to be attached to the external expression as such. The external expression has got to have something to express. The external may awaken the internal, may come as a fitting outlet of the internal, may even gauge the quality of the internal, but it can never entirely take the place of the internal. If by some mental process of negation the Mass itself could be performed as an unprayed rite and not as an act of sacrifice, it would not be to the honour and glory of God. We are given, by God and by the Church, the form which our public worship is to take. It is a better form than any which we could have discovered for ourselves. All that remains for us is to pray ourselves into it.

"This is all very well," is the comment which springs to the lips, "but in that case prayer is no more than a sort of game. According to you there is no point in offering to God what He has got already, and all that happens in liturgical prayer is a return to Him of words and sounds and actions which He has inspired but which don't help us much either. It looks as if God is giving us toy bricks to play with." Not at all. Certainly God provides us with the medium, but He also provides us with the purpose. The purpose is to please Him. In our liturgical prayer we are at least building a house to the glory of His name. There have to be bricks because we happen to be made with fingers. The angels are provided

with another sort of material for praise. Angels are pure spirit,
we are not. The angels build a wholly spiritual house, we
do not. Our house is part material because we are part material. But the building of it is no mere game. It is the highest use of the faculties and forms which He gives us. Indeed
it is the appropriate and perfectly harmonious use—in that
it is the highest combination—of the faculties and forms He
gives us.

Whether it is the priest at the altar or the monk in his
choir-stall or the layman who is following the liturgy at a
distance, the prayer which goes up to God is the return to
its Creator of the best which He has created. It is a restatement of the Word, a redirection to the source and term of
everything that is. "Dans le ronronnement de la psalmodie,"
writes Dom de Grunne,[1] "la spirale des images, des figurants
et des sentiments s'absorbe en un point unique: le Dieu de
Transcendance qui pénètre l'âme du croyant, la détache de
ces adhérences, l'élève, transcende les passions, transcende
les créatures et plane sur les frontières. Comme toute mu-
sique et toute poésie, les psaumes ont pour fonction d'intro-
duire ceux qui chantent dans un état spirituel qui est ici la
communion au Transcendant." This is surely the point—that
the parts are merged in the whole. Not only are they more
in communion with one another than at any other time, but
that, when they join in liturgical worship, they are one
breath with the voice of the Spirit. "Le moine," Dom de
Grunne goes on, "communie à Dieu par leurs symboles et
leur rythme en attendant de communier à lui par le pain et
le vin. Le sacrement poétique prépare le sacrement réel."

The perfect expression of all this is to be seen in the death
of the great Benedictine historian, St. Bede. To die while
singing the Magnificat antiphon "O Rex gloriae" with the
community on the feast of the Ascension is in the best possible tradition. With his last breath he kept the song going.

[1] In *Esprit et Vie,* April 1949.

Obviously if the whole purpose of human effort is taken to be natural well-being—or even moral goodness—then liturgical prayer must seem to be the grossest possible waste of time. But the purpose of human effort includes something more: in taking into account the supernatural it posits the need for a set form of public worship. A *set* form, and a *public* form. If the human purpose is for man and not merely for individual men, then there must be a form of expression which is suitable to the generality of mankind and not merely to the particular case. The need to express praise, penitence, gratitude and so on is answered in the liturgy: man has a vehicle: the channel of correspondence is provided. Private devotions may satisfy the single member, but it is only a set form of public worship which can satisfy that which he is a single member *of*.

To say that public worship makes no direct contribution towards the well-being of man and is therefore—from the point of view of furthering the main purpose—not worth doing is to make two entirely separate mistakes. In the first place, as we have already suggested, the sole end of man is not his welfare on earth whether physical or moral. While perfectly ready to grant that temporal good is a good and not an evil, we still reserve the right to claim that it is a good which must be related to other, and more important, goods. Where even moral good is divorced from supernatural good—and in the measure that it is so isolated—it ceases to have bearing upon the main purpose of man. Such, then, is the first error. The second is to mistake the function of the liturgy itself.

Now the whole idea of the liturgy is not to promote, directly, either well-being or uprightness. The idea is so to employ certain faculties and satisfy certain natural (and, as we shall see, supernatural) instincts in man that God is thereby worshipped according to His demands and that some of the debt for sin is paid according to His due. Primarily the

THE SOCIAL VALUE OF THE LITURGY 133

liturgy affects God, not us. In paying homage we therefore do a twofold thing and we obey a twofold instinct: we are being, for once, the complete man.

An example of how the natural and supernatural appetite work together in the act of praying publicly is to be seen in the sense of dual satisfaction which comes to the soul who discovers religion only after having reached the age of reason. Illustrations are numerous, but listen to the account of Thomas Merton's experience as it appears in his *Elected Silence:* "One came out of the church with a kind of comfortable and satisfied feeling that something had been done which needed to be done, and that was all I knew about it. And now, as I consider it after many years, I see that it was very good that I should have got at least that much of religion in my childhood. It is a law of man's nature, written into his very essence, *that he should want to stand together with other men in order to acknowledge their common dependence on God, their Father and Creator.*" The italics are mine.

If the intuitive sense of kinship with one's fellow man can be denied, so also can the intuitive sense of one's dependence upon God. Indeed the best way to blunt the one is to go ahead and blunt the other. The two hang together. Consequently the best way to develop each is to develop both. Common worship engenders compassion where there was no compassion before. To establish oneself as an untouchable—either in one's religion or in one's relation towards other people—is to sunder the bond which both nature and supernature have established between the members of the human race. Nothing brings this out so clearly as the implication of the liturgy. Very often it is through the liturgy that souls come to see that they are meant to find their way to God— indeed *can* only find their way to God—by means of others and in the company of others.

There is in Bath a stretch of public garden which is within waving distance of the railway. Few people, as a fact, wave from here because for some reason not many of the in-

habitants seem to have discovered it. Perhaps they prefer
to listen to the band. Here, then, in this seclusion, when
having to wait some time for either a train or an appoint-
ment with the dentist, I am accustomed to sit. I work, I
say Office, I read, I wave at trains.

Into what I have come to look upon as my own private
enclosure, came, some weeks ago, a small boy of some six or
seven years old. Under each arm he carried a white card-
board shoe-box. The boxes did not, as it turned out, contain
shoes; they contained a train. The engine in one box: metal
rails and signal in the other. Having fitted together the line
and laid it out on the grass, having adjusted the points and
wound up the engine, the little boy defeated the theory that
all children are perfectly happy playing endlessly by themselves by coming over to me and asking, with one finger on
the wheel of his engine to act as a brake, if I would care to
join in. So of course I put away my breviary, and assumed
the various roles which were assigned to me. The reason I
mention this trivial incident is that though playing trains
was well worth doing on that occasion (as indeed it mostly
is) the game only really reached its fullness when a real life-
sized train rattled past. Though our own locomotive was lost
in the roar, we were somehow given the note. We puffed
and whistled with confidence and conviction. We became
part of the British Railways.

So it is, in a way, with the liturgy. We become absorbed
into what is altogether bigger than ourselves. We allow our
own piping voices to be drowned in the universal roar of
prayer. Surely this should free our worship from many of
those elements of self which tend to spoil the note of our
more private and interior prayers? If this is true for the priest
or layman who is faithful to his rubrics, it is all the more
true of the religious who chants or recites the Divine Office
in choir. For the monk and nun—for all who tie themselves
by obedience to a regular observance—the pace, the pitch,
the required movements are a discipline. Even the times at
which the particular hours are said, and the place in choir

from which they are said, are outside the scope of personal choice. Self is sacrificed to service. The part is swallowed up in the whole. God is dictating the way in which He wants to be praised. Man is throwing in his lot with those who accept His dictation.

The Gospel paradox, then, applies once more: it is again a case of the seed having to die first if it is to have any sort of real life. We have to die to self in order to live for others; even our prayer must be swamped if it is truly to come into its own.

What is the good, they ask, of all those psalms and ceremonies? How is the world going to benefit—especially if the demands of liturgical and contemplative prayer may well involve retirement from the responsibilities of the world? Surely the natural comes first? If there is such a thing as the supernatural, it must wait. There is quite enough to attend to in this life without having to anticipate the exercises of the next. . . .

But surely the proper element of man is that which recognises his aspirations—not that which denies at least half, and those the nobler, of them. The rightly ordered man should feel at home in the liturgy. However badly he may pray, he feels that this is something appropriate to his being. His psalm, his chant—they are part of his language. Yes, but what is the *good* of such a language? Why not save your words and speak to men who need them? Why not preach in a language men understand?

The liturgy does preach. The effects may be indirect, but the sermon goes out from the choir-stall as surely as from the pulpit. However enclosed the religious order—indeed we would hold that the more enclosed the more effective is the sermon—the word of God goes out from the choir to all mankind. Each religious stands under a sounding-board which sends God's inspired sentences over the whole world, and, more important still, sends them to take their place in the choirs of heaven.

THE SONG OF CONTEMPLATION

It would be a mistake to think of contemplation *simply* as a song without words—just as it would be wrong to think of vocal prayer as being words without thought. Contemplative prayer may or may not make use of the form of words—ordinarily it feels happier without—and vocal prayer is equally free in the mental applications which it attaches to the words expressed. Apart from the obvious outward difference between the kind of prayer which makes a noise and the kind which is silent, it is idle to try and define the distinction absolutely. You cannot say that vocal prayer carries the soul to a certain precise point in the life of the spirit, and that after this the way is clear for contemplation. The contemplative, if he is praying properly, contemplates while he is singing the Divine Office: his imagination and memory are stilled, his intellect and will are bent upon God, his body is occupied in expressing praise. Here, certainly, is not a song without words—though it *is* a song in which the words take second place. Vocal prayer is here, under the impulse of contemplation, a mixed exercise of high perfection. Liturgical prayer, then, is the appropriate outward voice of the contemplative.

But whereas vocal prayer leans upon an activity of the mind, mental prayer does not depend in the same way upon words. (Indeed in its private prayer the soul has often to dispense with words—not because it despises them but because it feels them to be getting in the way.) The normal function of words in prayer is to express. Contemplation expresses without the use of words. The thought does not have to be explained, the petition does not have to be formulated. The sentiments of prayer no longer need a frame. This is far from suggesting that in its upward flight to God, the soul can now discard the liturgy: it is merely to suggest that the soul is able—outside the times of liturgical worship as well as inside those times—to pray contemplatively. Perhaps even more than before—and certainly not less—the soul feels the need of liturgical worship. But it is not tied to that one form of prayer. Souls of contemplation do not grow out of the Divine Office; they grow into it. And it grows into them. Their more direct elevation towards God gives to their vocal prayer a new force. It is the power which thought gives to action.

It is perhaps conceivable that action may be graceful without thought, may be dignified, may be elevating, may be challenging. But without thought it can hardly be meritorious; it can hardly be sanctifying. Thought is always bound to be purer than the action of which it is the inspiration, more significant than the phrase which formulates it. For example scientific research is possible only because there is something to search into and because there are minds to search with. The process is strictly a re-search. In the same way the more scientific forms of prayer, whether liturgical or discursive, are conditioned by the interior exercise of which they are the manifestation.

Now if the more interior forms of prayer are neglected or felt to have no practical bearing upon the world at large —that is to say if either the contemplative element is not taken into account in the running of the universe or if in the individual case there is no respect for the more abstract degrees of prayer—then not only does mankind as a whole suffer but the body of homage which goes up from man to God is impoverished. Where interior prayer is sacrificed to action, there is inevitably a weakening of the intensity of prayer all round. The more outward expressions of prayer, both in the individual soul and in the mass of souls, are to some extent devalued. Prayer, of whatever degree, is always meritorious, always *some* sort of expression of love; so as long as man prays at all he is enriching the world in which he lives and at the same time disposing himself for further grace. But in proportion as he allows extraversion and multiplicity to substitute for the interior response which his prayer invites him to give to God, he reduces the quality of his praise.

If applied mathematics recognises its debt to pure mathematics, you may be sure that applied prayer cannot afford to discard pure prayer. The one emerges out of the other, refers back to the other, derives its impetus from the other. It is not a case of which is more necessary or more excellent —because in this particular matter the objective may not be dissociated from the subjective without losing its terms of reference—it is a case of both working together in harmony. The word bears out the idea, the idea assumes the word.

The classic example of the way in which the principle may be perfected in practice is, of course, that of the nun in St. Teresa's community who knew no "mental prayer" *as such,* but who had contemplated for years with the material supplied by the Our Father.

A further error must be avoided. We must realise that the value of contemplation does not rest on the need for providing a quarry of thought to dig from and make into the material of the more scientific forms of prayer. Contemplation does not exist for the benefit of a system: it exists for the benefit of God. The song of contemplation is a song in its own right—sung for the ears of God. For us it is difficult to think of a song without words or notes, yet this is what contemplation is. And presumably even in the case of songs as we know them, songs which we hear sung, there is something present in the mind before there is anything which is capable of being written down in the score.

It is true, of course, that contemplation stores up spiritual energy which is later expended in more active work of one kind or another, and it is also true that but for the cells of contemplation which in every age are dotted about somewhere on the surface of the globe there can be no real progress, but all this has to do rather with contemplation's nature and effects than with its primary purpose.[1] The function of contemplation is more than that of recharging batteries. It is the battery and the dynamo in one—God getting the first benefit from it.

[1] And will be dealt with when we come to discuss the social value of contemplation.

The bid which we are making in these pages for what might be called "integral contemplation" may seem utterly out of place in a book which is chiefly designed for people living in the world who find it difficult enough to make room in their day for straightforward vocal and discursive prayer. We make it nevertheless. The present intention is to break down the prejudice against the more interior forms of prayer which exists in the minds of active souls. After nearly two thousand years Martha is still suspicious of Mary. And we can hardly blame her: there is evidence to show for active prayer—let alone the active life—while there is none at all for secret contemplation. Yet once we lose sight of the fact that integral is of more value than applied prayer there is nothing to prevent the whole business of prayer degenerating into a scientific, analytical, effect-producing, ego-bound process of research. It need not become this, but such is the danger. Pure contemplation is as far above analytical method as history is above historical criticism, as Scripture is above exegesis.

By all means let those souls who genuinely feel themselves called to active ways of prayer, and who are not confusing humility with laziness, stick to their attraction and go ahead. It will bring them very close to God, and they will also be able to teach to other people much of what they have learned in prayer. But let those who feel drawn to a quieter, more recollective, less vocal exercise be on their guard against trying to pigeon-hole the process. Nothing is more destructive of the spirit of pure prayer than the effort to check up. To a large extent the song of contemplation depends for its purity upon the soul's willingness to forget about its own experience, its degree of achievement, its handling of counterpoint. Even if this self-analysis does not lead to making a culture of spirituality—and armchair contemplation is worse than useless—it gives rise to scrupulosity and nerves. Clearly in proportion as self becomes the object of investigation the soul's gaze upon God is deflected. Which gets us back to the fundamental truth about prayer, that nothing—neither aesthetic appreciation, technical proficiency, metaphysical specu-

lation, affective emotion nor anything else—does service for
the end of prayer itself.

Worship is the finest song that can be sung, and there will
always be men and women in the world to sing it. There may
not be many, but there will be some. If the rest of the world
is deaf to the melody, the loss is the world's. For those who
are granted to hear, and still more, of course, for those who
are themselves granted to sing, there are weighty obligations.
If it for Martha, understanding the principle of the thing at
last, to justify to the world the existence of Mary; while it is
for Mary, conscious of her responsibility, to come in her own
way to the assistance of Martha. *Contemplata aliis tradere.*
All too easily, and almost as it were through muddle-head-
edness rather than through downright malice, can the song
of contemplation be drowned. Either the worker can work so
unsparingly as not to spare a thought for the life of the spirit,
or the spiritual soul can despair of ever being able to achieve
anything by the sheer spirituality of his effort. For both there
is the need for great faith. In the contemplative the need is
even greater than in the active, because in the contemplative
the sense of futility is both more keen and more constant
than in the active. The active soul can escape from the
thought of its own insufficiency; the contemplative is living
right up against it all the time. There comes a point in the
development of the spiritually enlightened man when it seems
that the whole effort has been absolutely useless, wasted.
Nothing of what has been learned can possibly be imparted
to others, so what is the good of trying? The light has been too
strong: it has blinded. "I will retire into my own cocoon and
live as far as possible in the spirit. I cannot bear the thought
of what the world needs to learn. The whole thing is too
big for me. I dare not, expressing myself so badly, do battle with the armies of ignorance and malice and unbelief."

Was the song, then, for the ears of the singer only? Is this
all that was meant in the terms of the commission—that the
voice should remain behind closed doors? Even granted that
the sum of the contemplative's knowledge is in the end something inexpressible in human language—or expressible only in

formulas which sound trite enough to all except the soul himself, and to him are charged with meaning—it belongs to a Wisdom which may not be silenced. Even if, like Moses and Ezechiel, he can only stammer, the contemplative has no right to content himself with remaining merely dumb. He must try. If he gets no further than telling the world that he knows nothing whatever, that all created things are shadows, and that nothing matters on this earth except trying to unite oneself more and more with the Will of God, he will not have done so badly. The saints themselves have very little more to tell us when they come to die. These things are true, and there is not much to add. So let us go on proclaiming them. We sing while there's voice left.

THE SERENITY OF CONTEMPLATION

A thought which probably comes to the mind of the reader who goes straight on from the previous page is that if the song of contemplation is as here described, it must be an exceedingly simple and short song. In substance it certainly is, but it goes on to the last and often it is a remarkably painful thing to keep up. Indeed apart from the grace of God which makes it possible in the first place it can only be kept up by the practice of a deliberate and conscientious serenity: one must refuse to be disturbed by disappointment, one must maintain a studied indifference to success or failure. Thus it might be said that while the conditions of contemplation are generosity and perseverance, while its climate is self-denial, and while its effects are trust and humility, the particular quality which runs through all three aspects of contemplation is that of serenity. Which is why contemplative prayer comes so hardly to the world of today: we have lost the power of being serene.

In an age which has left the study of spiritual, metaphysical, transcendental things to the very few, and has concentrated the vast preponderance of its effort on the physical sciences, there has to be, before any sort of return to Christian values can be effected, a restatement of prayer's fundamental postulates. The value and primary purpose of prayer have at least to be recognised before anything can be expected at all. It is a vicious circle: Western civilisation has become so materialistic that it cannot see the point of prayer, and unless it prays it never will. Having lost the knack of praying, it has lost the knack of being serene. And unless it decides so to keep its materialism in check as to allow for a greater serenity it can never be master of its own so-called progress. Without prayer, without serenity, the West must continue to rattle downhill.[1]

I remember once seeing a Poor Clare sitting in the station at Calais. In that shouting, hot, pushing, cosmopolitan crowd she looked as if she had been dropped from another planet. There she sat on her wicker suitcase, hands folded, cool, unflustered, serene. *Non movebitur in aeternum*—it was a Thursday and I had just been saying Prime. More out of curiosity, I regret to say, than from a Christian charity I went over and asked if I could show her into her train. It appeared she had no particular train in mind; any train would do so long as it was going in the right direction. She had missed several; there was no hurry. "Thank you, I think I'll wait", she said, "until things settle down a little." When I told her she would have to wait forty or fifty years, until everyone travelled by air, she asked quite simply, "Oh, is it always like this? People are so excited, I thought there must have been an accident." She was middle-aged, and had not been away from her convent since she had joined as a girl of seventeen. I did not say so, because it would have taken too long to explain, but, of course, she was right: there *had* been an accident. The Western races were suffering the effects of the accident of materialism. And it is doubtful whether they will ever recover. But that was why she looked so out of place: in her convent she had been travelling at a different speed and by

[1] What the chances are in the East for a redirection of civilisation is another matter, and will be touched upon briefly below.

a quite different route: she had by-passed the scene of the catastrophe. You might carry the idea further and say that she had come upon the evidence of the wreckage and not known what it was all about. Indeed it is doubtful whether any of us really appreciate the extent of the damage. The nun saw the excitement and rush, possibly also the greed and uncharity and general hardness, and was puzzled by it. Not unduly disturbed, merely puzzled. *Quare fremuerunt gentes, et meditati sunt inania?* Why indeed—when the consequences are found to be so disastrous?

In other words the atmosphere is all wrong for the Poor Clare kind of prayer which we have been considering. The wind is in a completely different direction, and is blowing contemplation out of Europe. Whether it is blowing it out of America as well it is not so easy, at the present time, to say. Presumably it must be—since it is the same wind. Of all materialist societies it is true to say with the Psalmist: *Contritio et infelicitas in viis eorum et viam pacis non cognoverunt; non est timor Die ante oculos eorum.* Of course they are anxious and harassed and are afraid: they have nothing in which they can place their trust. When even earthly securities are seen to fail, men must snatch at what little they can find in compensation. The only things left, once God has been crowded out and the satisfactory handling of His universe has been despaired of, are the merest toys. Hence greed, nerves, suspicion, fear. *Dominum non invocaverunt; illic trepidaverunt timore, ubi non erat timor.*

This means that what came more or less naturally to men in the ages of faith, because the faculty was inherited and the atmosphere was conducive, has now to be forced—as though it were a hot-house growth, which it is not—if it is to be preserved at all. Contemplation ought not to be in danger of becoming self-conscious, rare, specialist. If its function were recognised by the world this danger would not exist. Thus both for its own sake and for the world's, let alone for God's sake, the sooner contemplation can find again an accepted place in the scheme of creation the better.

To the Eastern mind there is not this same difficulty. The

psychology of the East has not been affected by industrialism. Industrialism is still not only alien but recognised as inimical to the whole spirit of the Eastern tradition. The culture of the East has so far shown itself to be impervious to Western influences and has consequently preserved much of what we have lost. Even the most superficial study of Oriental thought must convince the reader, as it has convinced the present writer, that if Christian contemplation is to see a revival it is far more likely to be in China or in India than in Europe or America. Anyone who accepts the challenging implications of Dom Pierre-Célestin Lou Tseng-Tsiang's book, *Ways of Confucius and of Christ*,[2] and who further examines the Chinese, Hindu and Buddhist ideologies cannot but be struck by the comparison between the present state of the world and the period immediately preceding the coming of the Gospel. What, in the Providence of God, the Greek philosophers were doing to prepare the way for the birth of Christian theology and philosophy in the West, Eastern thought seems, over a far longer period, to be doing by the way of preparation for its extension. Rome is not above being helped by Buddha and Confucius any more than it is above being helped by Plato and Aristotle. Anyone who is interested in the possibilities of this idea should read what the Jesuit Fathers who are working in India have to say about it. We in this country have for far too long taken up the complacent attitude that no serious thinking is done east of, say, Jerusalem. The works of Johanns, Dandoy, Fuchs, and Narayan (to mention only a few which are easily accessible) should disabuse us of this error.

Philosophy and contemplation have never been able to dispense with each other's services, and it should be humbling as well as encouraging to us to see that they are still working in close harmony in the East. If what they are both lacking is the Incarnation it may be the mission of present-

[2] Burns & Oates, 1948. Dom Pierre-Célestin, who died shortly after writing the book, was a monk of Saint-André, the Benedictine Abbey near Bruges. A convert from Confucianism, he had held office both as Ambassador and Foreign Minister.

day Christianity to bring it to them. Certainly the dispositions are there. All it wants are saints. Again and again we have had evidence that the most potent argument to the Oriental mind is sanctity. Contemplative and liturgical prayer are understood: the tranquil Eastern temperament respects the withdrawn life of worship, and is slightly suspicious of proselytising activity. Dom Pierre-Célestin Lou's belief that it is to be St. Benedict's Rule which will ultimately bring his people to the grace of conversion is by no means a mere partisan monkish fancy. He knows both sides from within.

Some of this may appear discouraging to those who think that Christian contemplation, the Christian tradition even, once planted in Europe may one day have to be uprooted and transferred to another continent. The thought of this possibility should not be so very discouraging when we consider that the same sort of thing has happened before without essential loss to the Church. Who, at the time, would have believed that the Christian schools of Alexandria, Constantinople, Antioch would ever be closed? What Christian of that period would have envisaged without fear for the whole structure of contemporary religion the withdrawal of contemplation from the great strongholds of solitary prayer, the deserts of Syria and North Africa? And yet Christian thought survived, the solitary life sprang up elsewhere. As a fact contemplation derived new impulse rather than otherwise from the direction given to monachism by the change. No, we in Western Europe today need have no worries about the fate of Christianity in general or of Christian contemplation in particular. Our Lord did not say: "I will be with you always, even to the consummation of the world—in Western Europe." *Somewhere* the Church and the mystical life will go on; in one place or another souls will be uniting themselves to Christ in the closest possible relationship known to man, and that is all that matters.

We should think of the whole business of contemplation as a great eagle soaring above the activities of men and carrying the precious grains of prayer in its beak. Every now and then a grain of contemplation is dropped, but you can

never be quite sure where it is going to land. Sometimes it is
carried by the wind far out of the eagle's course. But this does
not matter. He will, like the little nun on her wicker suitcase in the busy French port, arrive eventually. It will strike
root and grow where God wants it to. This kind of seed has
the quality of coming up in the most unlikely places; it has
even the quality of being planted in one place and appearing
in another. There is no telling. Africa, Europe, America, Asia?
Perhaps it is Asia's turn.[3]

Be this as it may about the geography of contemplation,
there can be no doubt about its psychological requirements:
we get back again to the need of a mental, and even an outward, tranquillity. In the individual soul as well as in the
world at large it is the steady noiseless flame which keeps up
the temperature of exterior activity. Take away the silent
tongue of fire from under the kettle and the busy bubbling
surface cools. The temperature of the water depends not
upon what looks the most active but upon what looks entirely
static. The disturbance of the water's surface is no more
than a sign: it is the intensity of the flame, which in turn depends upon the quality of the spirit, that matters. The working of the spirit-lamp would seem misleading to anyone who
knew nothing of the ways of heat: so also is the working of
contemplation to those who know nothing of tranquillity.

[3] Having come to the end of such passages in this book as refer
to contemporary and comparative religions, I would like to
acknowledge with gratitude some of the authorities which have
proved helpful. Apart from Dom Pierre-Célestin Lou Tseng-
Tsiang's book frequently mentioned (*Ways of Confucius and of
Christ*) I am chiefly indebted to the following: *Introduction to the
Vedanta* and *A Synopsis of 'To Christ through the Vedanta'* by
P. Johanns, S.J.; *The Way and its Power, A Study of the Tao Te
Ching and its place in Chinese Thought* by Arthur Waley; *The
Great Synthesis* by Stephen Fuchs; *L'Ontologie du Vedanta* by G.
Dandoy, S.J.; *A Preface to Prayer* by Gerald Heard; *Platonisme et
Théologie Mystique* by Jean Daniélou; "Bouddhisme et Chris-
tianisme" in *Témoignages*, Jan. 1949: and lastly to Dom Bede
Griffiths, prior of Farnborough, who opened up the subject for me
and told me what to read.

Because tranquillity is something positive it is something which has to be deliberately cultivated: we generate serenity, paradoxical as it may sound, in the same way that we generate energy. That is to say we carefully store it up and then carefully expend it. But always we expend it serenely. "We tend nowadays to think of silence as the privation of sound," says Fr. Gerald Vann,[4] "whereas it is noise that is the privation of silence. If we want to watch with Christ and live with Christ we must learn first to be still. Throughout the Passion there are these enclaves of silence against the background of noise and tumult; and the sound and fury signify nothing but death, produce nothing but futility: it is the silence that is creative of life."

This idea of the productive power of stillness is profoundly true, and unless we grasp it we can never hope to see deeply into the qualities of which it is the disposition. "Be still," urges Jeremias, "and see that the Lord is God." Be still, and see what is wrong about the movements in which we of this generation are becoming dangerously involved. "In that stillness," says Fr. Vann, "and only there, humanity as a whole will find new heart."

When souls are at the mercy of chance disturbance, and know themselves to be so, there can be no true spirit of prayer. The sense of balance, if it is to be a lasting state and not merely the condition occasioned by having things where you want them, must be achieved. Excited nerves may be calmed down, but they do not stay calm unless a settled and creative peace is introduced. Greed and anxiety are the disturbing elements, and it requires a more astringent solution than a few pious practices and devotions if the soul is to become detached and free from fear: the soul has to be disinfected with the quiet deliberate search for God in all the circumstances of life. To quote the same authority for the last time: "Sanctity has been defined as simply 'willing what happens to us by God's order' . . . it is this that would finally and inevitably give us peace, because it would give us still-

[4] In a broadcast during Holy Week 1949, printed later in *Life of the Spirit* (Vol. IV, No. 37).

ness and serenity . . . and so the futility and the fear would finally be driven out." If to will what happens to us by God's order makes necessarily for holiness, then it is equally true that to contemplate makes necessarily for such a disposition of will.

THE SOCIAL VALUE OF CONTEMPLATION

From what has been said it may be gathered that contemplation is not a mere private hobby. Just as when you think of the union of the soul with Christ you think immediately of the communion of the soul with other people, so when you have discussed the serenity of contemplatives you think at once of what value the act of contemplation is to other people. Our purpose here is to show that the activity of contemplation is more dynamic than any other.

We have seen that for the ordinary soul it is impossible, short of intuitive comprehension which would be an exceptional grace, to appreciate the inwardness of life in the natural order. The meaning of creation is opened out to the soul in the measure that the soul can come to look upon creation through the eyes of God. In other words it is the direct and unbeglamoured vision of creatures as they really are that gives to the contemplative his effectiveness: not only does he see all creation as in its source, namely God, but he is sufficiently detached from the selfish approach to it as to be a willing instrument in its service. If God loves His creation as having its origin and end in Himself, man's love of creation is correspondingly more unselfish and more effective in proportion as he comes to see its source and term in God. Which is precisely what the contemplative does come to see. Everything about life is, to the true mystic, explainable only in terms of God.

It is thus part of the assimilated knowledge which his prayer has afforded him that there is no contradiction in the scheme of creation as viewed by the soul of truly interior Christian prayer. That this is the case in specifically Christian prayer is worth noting because it is precisely on the relationship between Creator and His creatures that non-Christian contemplation goes wrong. Mysticism outside the Church tends either to one or other extreme: believing on the one hand that the universe emanates from God and is actually part of Him,[1] and on the other that only the spiritual sphere is real and that its material manifestation is a delusion of the senses.[2] It is only the Christian doctrine that can bridge the gulf, and it is therefore only the Christian mystic who does not have to do violence to himself in order to wrest his attention from the object to the object's origin and end. He does so instinctively in virtue of his Christian contemplative habit.

The more his window of prayer is opened the more does the visible world tell to the contemplative about the horizons of God. Knowing more about the world than we do, the contemplative is more concerned about its welfare than we are. He is all the more eager, but more selflessly eager, to bring it help. His whole effort—the only activity he is any good at, namely his contemplative effort—goes into the work of saving the world for God. Prayer is the contribution which it is specifically his to make. He makes it—to God and for man.

"Yes, I see all that," you may say, "but how am I to know that it is the smallest use? I'm not saying that it isn't very nice of the contemplative to give us the benefit of his ecstasies and so on, but what is there to prove that they do in fact benefit us?" The answer is that if you believe in the efficacious merits of Christ, you should believe too, in the efficacy of those merits which lie closest to those of Christ. Since Christ's prayer is not a private and restricted prayer, neither is that of the mystic. The soul which is united to

[1] Pantheism (or, more strictly, the form of Pantheism which is called Theopantism).

[2] Idealism.

Christ is united to His prayer, and the two prayers go out over the world and up to the Father as one.

Accordingly we can claim that not only is prayer *a* way in which a man may help his fellow men but it is *the best* way. If the Prayer and Passion of Christ is the way chosen by God for man's assistance, then incorporation in Christ by prayer and suffering is the way most suited to man for mutual assistance. In prayer man is granted to share with God in a re-creative and re-redemptive work. The contemplative, more than any of his fellows, helps to support the universe which God has created and continues to conserve. He is the instrument, the fulcrum, which God has chosen for the sustaining of the world. This is an idea much favoured by spiritual writers, and it is well worth thinking about. But it is likely to be dismissed as a pious fancy unless some sort of substantiation can be advanced. Perhaps the best way of approaching it is by the use of a simile.

Recalling the legend about the king who grew to be so fond of gold paint that he painted himself all over with it and then died of suffocation, we can see in the function of contemplation a work comparable to that of breathing through the pores of the skin. Just as no amount of extra breathing through the mouth and nose can do service for the pores' contribution to the life of the human body, so no amount of extra activity can do service for the function of contemplation in the life of the body of mankind. As a breathing apparatus the pores of the skin are not as obviously effective as the nose and mouth, yet if the world should ever manage to block up those unobtrusive little mystical passages which never cease to inhale and send out the spirit of true prayer[3] it would not be long before outward progress ceased. Lacking the assistance of something which, in the plan of creation, it is necessary for the world to possess, a completely non-contemplative and anti-interior civilisation must inevitably go to pieces. Perhaps this will explain what writers like Merton

[3] Or cover them over with gold which would have the same effect.

and others mean—though it cannot prove that what they say is true—when they claim that it is the minute amount of mysticism in the world which keeps the rest of the thing together, and that but for the ordered prayer of the few there would be chaos and disorder for the many. Certain it is that were it not for the constant tradition of a strictly interior life within the Church, the purely silent feeding of the lungs with grace, there would be nothing at all in the way of outward voice.

It is the old story of the active life depending on the contemplative, the wheels going round because of the hidden energy somewhere else, Martha being kept going by Mary who looks half asleep. Familiar as all this is as a theme to those who have grown up in the Catholic way of thought, it is neither easy to act upon in practice nor acceptable even in theory by the world at large. It requires the act of faith.

What we have to realise, in such a way that for us it becomes a truth for every day, is that once a soul enters the world of the spirit it begins to live in a new dimension which not only defies measurement by the physical sciences but which also eludes even the human intelligence enlightened by grace. It may be tested by obedience and by a number of signs both interior and exterior, but it is *measurable* only by God. This being so, it is idle to spend the whole of one's endeavour upon searching and weighing up. The only profitable course is to trust, ask forgiveness, and go on blindly trying to love.

WE LIVE, WORK, SING, AND DIE

It seems suitable, having marched with hymns and banner round the four sides of the square,[1] to finish up on a note which has been struck repeatedly throughout the procession.

[1] *We Live with Our Eyes Open, We Work while the Light Lasts, We Sing while There's Voice Left, We Die Standing Up.*

Again and again it must be insisted that the spiritual life is part of the universal vocation, and that for most people it is even in this life the only solution. Having grasped the idea that conformity with God's will is the only thing that is really worth while, what next? "Oh yes, it means planning one's day so that it is broken up with various devotions, it means doing without comforts and possessions and friendships, it means going about doing good and looking awful and feeling full of those frightful interior desolations." Surely not. Though holiness may involve some of these things, the essentials of holiness are far more fundamental. They deserve enumeration once again.

In the first place there is the distinction beween planning one's day for God and living one's life for Him. The saint is the man who makes God his sole aim in life: his *day* falls into line. In the same way his relationships, his pleasures, his use of earthly things take their colour from the object of his desire. Everything is weighed up in terms of that. The man of God lives, works, sings and dies for God. And in doing so he lives, works, sings and dies for man. There can be nothing departmental in the approach of one who gives all and aims at the One.

Having got his soul orientated, the man who is searching for God in the far distance of heaven must realise that he can find Him in the closest intimacy—in Christ. If he seeks for any other kind of union with God, apart from Christ, he had better forget that he had ever started and begin again with a copy of the Gospels in his hands. It is only when the Incarnation is grasped as being the basis of the soul's relationship with the Father that the disposition for true Christian mysticism can be properly said to exist. Love of Christ *is* true Christian mysticism. And nothing else is.

Which brings us to the question as to how far any sort of true Christian mysticism, however undeveloped, may come within the capacity of the ordinary Christian soul. Now if we have defined the quality as love of Christ, we obviously mean that all are called to walk in that way. To begin to love our Lord is to begin upon a course which, given grace and fidelity, is designed to proceed to Divine Union. We must all begin to love our Lord. What is claimed here is that many more could proceed to Divine Union in this life than in actual fact do so proceed. And as a reason for the deficiency we would suggest that the spiritual life is looked upon as an extra or specialised interest for the few and not as part of the general vocation for the many. The harmfulness of this view lies in the fact that it has come, in practice, to be very nearly true. A paragraph will explain what is meant.

It is a fact that people do not go in for the interior life as they used to: the majority are satisfied with their devotions, and there is a dwindling minority. Consequently those who do go in for the life of contemplation are, from being habitually thought of as performing a work of supererogation, forced into a somewhat false position: they are in danger of imagining that they are conferring a singular benefit upon mankind—which in a sense is true—and that they must stand high in the favour of God for carrying on in a work which brings little or no human recognition. When the contemplative loses the feel of normality about his vocation, he is in danger of losing his sense of direction as well. It does not do for the soul to consider what sort of a return he is getting for his interior labours. He must work in order to please God, and the recognition which he gets from creatures is beside the point. That he benefits the human race is, as we have seen at some length, assured: that he pleases God is, again, certain. But in whose favour he stands, and whether the degree be high or low, is none of his business. From what has been said it may seem that the curve of contemplation, once it dips numerically, is likely to dip qualitatively as well, and that consequently it is of the greatest importance that souls should realise their responsibilities towards responding to the grace. If more people contemplated, fewer people would think self-consciously about their contemplation. And there would be more chance of everybody contemplating right.

One of the effects of the drift from the Christian tradition is the inability on the part of the non-praying mind to understand the idea behind the enclosed orders. The religious life is allowable where there is something to show for it; not otherwise. Then comes the well-meaning soul and explains that contemplation winds up the machine, prepares people for action, stores up energy . . . and so on. This is perfectly true but it does not go far enough: it must be realised that contemplation is an action in itself, indeed the highest action, and even if it did not prepare anyone for anything it would be supremely and infinitely worth while. Our ancestors in the faith understood this without having to be reminded of it: we, with the decay of spiritual sensibility and an alarming awareness of material things to take its place, have allowed a shifting of values within almost all the spiritual estimates. Instinctively we judge as the world judges, and only when faced with expressing our judgement do we hold up our opinion to the light of the spirit. Such is the effect which material things are having upon man that within the definition of things themselves, whether spiritual or moral or intellectual or physical, the emphasis is laid upon the accidental rather than upon the essential, the outward rather than upon the real.

Unless in the spiritual order we go the whole way and look for the real rather than rest satisfied with the obvious, we shall miss the whole point about prayer and love and self-sacrifice. The essential part about the life of faith is that it should not stop short at the obvious. It may sound obvious enough that we pray in order to be virtuous or in order to get what we want, but the truth is that we pray in order that the virtue of our prayer may be pleasing to God and that He may get what He wants. The other factors are secondary.

Thus, to conclude, the influence of prayer upon our characters and upon our work and upon our world is enormous. But it is not essentially intended to be formative. Essentially it is intended to be unitive. If its purpose were merely to train and educate, then outward things could be its test. But outward things are often not forthcoming at all where prayer is concerned.

"But," you will say, "we are always told that our action is purified by our prayer. You have said so yourself." Quite right: action can be not only purified but sanctified by prayer. But it would be a want of right emphasis to say that action is the main thing and that prayer must be dragged along as a sort of afterthought. Prayer has not been invented so as to keep action on the right lines. Prayer, particularly of course contemplation, has been invented so as to keep man acting in his right relation to God—namely by worshipping Him with the highest of his powers. Though it would be wrong to say that prayer is essential to the existence of action—because for one thing prayer could not be responsible for action which is bad—it would certainly not be wrong to say that prayer is its inspiration and safeguard. Far from action being the main thing and prayer its hanger-on, prayer is the main thing and action is its expression.

After so much in this book which lays stress upon prayer's necessity, and after so little which tells people how to pray, it is necessary in a concluding paragraph to admit that there can never in this life be a satisfactory solution to the problem of prayer. Acknowledge the need, attempt the undertaking with the grace of God, trust absolutely in Divine Wisdom, and do not turn back for anything in the world. This is the only formula. It will not be felt to work, but then the sense of failure is covered by its terms. The effort to fulfil it will help others as much as it will help oneself. But this will not be felt either. A rather dreary project? Not at all! It is the most challenging and tremendous that God can offer to the heart and mind of man. It is the invitation of Divine Love.

Image Books

... MAKING THE WORLD'S FINEST
CATHOLIC LITERATURE AVAILABLE TO ALL

Image Books

**. . . MAKING THE WORLD'S FINEST
CATHOLIC LITERATURE AVAILABLE TO ALL**

ON THE TRUTH OF THE
CATHOLIC FAITH
*Summa Contra Gentiles Book II:
Creation. Newly translated, with
an Introduction and notes by
James F. Anderson*   D27—95¢

ON THE TRUTH OF THE
CATHOLIC FAITH
*Summa Contra Gentiles Book
III: Providence. Newly trans-
lated, with an Introduction and
notes by Vernon J. Bourke*
      D28a Book III, Part 1—95¢
      D28b Book III, Part 2—95¢

ON THE TRUTH OF THE
CATHOLIC FAITH
*Summa Contra Gentiles Book
IV: Salvation. Newly translated,
with an Introduction and notes,
By Charles J. O'Neil*   D29—95¢

THE WORLD'S FIRST LOVE
By Fulton J. Sheen   D30—85¢

THE SIGN OF JONAS
By Thomas Merton   D31—95¢

PARENTS, CHILDREN AND THE
FACTS OF LIFE   *By Henry V.
Sattler, C.SS.R.*   D32—75¢

LIGHT ON THE MOUNTAIN:
*The Story of La Salette
By John S. Kennedy*   D33—75¢

EDMUND CAMPION
By Evelyn Waugh   D34—75¢

HUMBLE POWERS
By Paul Horgan   D35—75¢

SAINT THOMAS AQUINAS
By G. K. Chesterton D36—75¢

APOLOGIA PRO VITA SUA
*By John Henry Cardinal New-
man   Introduction by Philip
Hughes*   D37—95¢

A HANDBOOK OF THE CATHOLIC
FAITH
*By Dr. N. G. M. Van Doornik,
Rev. S. Jelsma, Rev. A. Van De
Lisdonk. Ed. Rev. John Green-
wood*   D38—$1.45

THE NEW TESTAMENT
Official Catholic edition
                       D39—95¢

MARIA CHAPDELAINE
By Louis Hémon   D40—65¢

SAINT AMONG THE HURONS
By Francis X. Talbot, S.J.
                       D41—95¢

THE PATH TO ROME
By Hilaire Belloc   D42—85¢

SORROW BUILT A BRIDGE
By Katherine Burton D43—85¢

THE WISE MAN FROM THE WEST
By Vincent Cronin   D44—85¢

EXISTENCE AND THE EXISTENT
By Jacques Maritain D45—75¢

THE STORY OF THE TRAPP
FAMILY SINGERS
By Maria Augusta Trapp
                       D46—95¢

THE WORLD, THE FLESH AND
FATHER SMITH
By Bruce Marshall   D47—75¢

THE CHRIST OF CATHOLICISM
By Dom Aelred Graham
                       D48—95¢

SAINT FRANCIS XAVIER
By James Brodrick, S.J.
                       D49—95¢

SAINT FRANCIS OF ASSISI
By G. K. Chesterton D50—65¢

11

Image Books

*...making the world's finest
Catholic literature available to all*

VIPERS' TANGLE
by François Mauriac   D51—75¢

THE MANNER IS ORDINARY
by John LaFarge, S.J. D52—95¢

MY LIFE FOR MY SHEEP
by Alfred Duggan   D53—90¢

**THE CHURCH AND THE RECONSTRUCTION OF THE MODERN
WORLD:** *The Social Encyclicals
of Pius XI.* Edited by T. P. McLaughlin, C.S.B.   D54—$1.25

A GILSON READER: *Selections from
the Writings of Etienne Gilson.*
Edited by Anton C. Pegis.
D55—$1.25

**THE AUTOBIOGRAPHY OF
ST. THERESE OF LISIEUX:** *The Story
of a Soul. A new translation by*
John Beevers.   D56—75¢

HELENA
by Evelyn Waugh   D57—75¢

THE GREATEST BIBLE STORIES
A Catholic Anthology from
World Literature. Edited by Anne
Fremantle.   D58—75¢

THE CITY OF GOD—St. Augustine.
Edited with Intro. by Vernon J.
Bourke. Foreword by Etienne
Gilson.   D59—$1.45

SUPERSTITION CORNER
by Sheila Kaye-Smith D60—65¢

SAINTS AND OURSELVES
Ed. by Philip Caraman, S.J.
D61—95¢

CANA IS FOREVER
by Charles Hugo Doyle
D62—75¢

**ASCENT OF MOUNT CARMEL—
St. John of the Cross.** Translated
and Edited by E. Allison Peers.
D63—$1.25

**RELIGION AND THE RISE OF
WESTERN CULTURE**
by Christopher Dawson
D64—85¢

**PRINCE OF DARKNESS AND OTHER
STORIES**
by J. F. Powers   D65—85¢

ST. THOMAS MORE
by E. E. Reynolds   D66—95¢

JESUS AND HIS TIMES
2 Volumes   D67A—95¢
by Daniel-Rops   D67B—95¢

ST. BENEDICT
by Justin McCann, O.S.B.
D68—85¢

THE LITTLE FLOWERS OF ST. FRANCIS
Edited and Translated by
Raphael Brown.   D69—95¢

THE QUIET LIGHT
by Louis de Wohl   D70—95¢

CHARACTERS OF THE REFORMATION
by Hilaire Belloc   D71—85¢

THE BELIEF OF CATHOLICS
by Ronald Knox   D72—75¢

FAITH AND FREEDOM
by Barbara Ward   D73—95¢

**GOD AND INTELLIGENCE IN
MODERN PHILOSOPHY**
by Fulton J. Sheen D74—$1.25

If your bookseller is unable to supply certain titles, write to Image
Books, Department MIB, Garden City, New York, stating the
titles you desire and enclosing the price of each book (plus 5¢
per book to cover cost of postage and handling). Prices are subject to change without notice.   21

Image Books

**... MAKING THE WORLD'S FINEST
CATHOLIC LITERATURE AVAILABLE TO ALL**

THE IDEA OF A UNIVERSITY
By John Henry Cardinal Newman. Introduction by George N. Shuster   D75—$1.45

PLAYED BY EAR: *The Autobiography of Father Daniel A. Lord, S.J.*   D76—95¢

MY BELOVED: *The Story of a Carmelite Nun. By Mother Catherine Thomas*   D77—75¢

DARK NIGHT OF THE SOUL
By St. John of the Cross. Edited and translated by E. Allison Peers   D78—75¢

TERESA OF AVILA
By Marcelle Auclair. Translated by Kathleen Pond   D79—$1.45

SAINT PETER THE APOSTLE
By William Thomas Walsh   D80—95¢

THE LOVE OF GOD
By Dom Aelred Graham, O.S.B.   D81—85¢

WOMAN OF THE PHARISEES
By François Mauriac. Translated by Gerard Hopkins   D82—75¢

THE PILLAR OF FIRE
By Karl Stern   D83—85¢

ORTHODOXY
By G. K. Chesterton   D84—75¢

THIS IS CATHOLICISM
By John J. Walsh   D85—$1.25

MEDIEVAL ESSAYS
By Christopher Dawson   D86—95¢

VESSEL OF CLAY
By Leo Trese   D87—65¢

SAINTS FOR SINNERS
By Alban Goodier, S.J.   D88—75¢

THE LONG LONELINESS
By Dorothy Day   D89—85¢

THIS IS THE MASS
By Henri Daniel-Rops. Photographs of Bishop Fulton J. Sheen by Karsh   D90—95¢

THE ORIGIN OF THE JESUITS
By James Brodrick, S.J.   D91—85¢

A POPULAR HISTORY OF THE REFORMATION
By Philip Hughes   D92—95¢

THE RESTLESS FLAME
By Louis de Wohl   D93—85¢

PROGRESS AND RELIGION
By Christopher Dawson   D94—85¢

THE CATHOLIC CHURCH IN THE MODERN WORLD
By E. E. Y. Hales   D95—95¢

THE LIFE OF TERESA OF JESUS:
The Autobiography of St. Teresa of Avila. Translated and with an introduction by E. Allison Peers   D96—$1.25

GIANTS OF THE FAITH
By John A. O'Brien   D97—95¢

SCHOLASTICISM AND POLITICS
By Jacques Maritain   D98—95¢

THE SON OF GOD
By Karl Adam   D99—85¢

THE MAN WHO WAS CHESTERTON
Edited by Raymond T. Bond   D100—$1.45

Image Books

... MAKING THE WORLD'S FINEST
CATHOLIC LITERATURE AVAILABLE TO ALL

**THE CONFESSIONS OF
ST. AUGUSTINE**
*Translated, with an introduction
and notes, by John K. Ryan*
D101—$1.25

HEART IN PILGRIMAGE
*By Evelyn Eaton and Edward
Roberts Moore* D102—75¢

THE HEART OF MAN
By Gerald Vann, O.P. D103—75¢

**BABY GROWS IN AGE AND
GRACE**
By Sister Mary de Lourdes
D104—75¢

**ESSAY ON THE DEVELOPMENT
OF CHRISTIAN DOCTRINE**
*By John Henry Cardinal Newman
Introduction by Gustave Weigel, S.J.*
D105—$1.35

**THE STORY OF AMERICAN
CATHOLICISM, 2 Volumes**
By Theodore Maynard
D106A—95¢
D106B—95¢

**THE CASE OF CORNELIA
CONNELLY**
By Juliana Wadham D107—85¢

UNDERSTANDING EUROPE
By Christopher Dawson
D108—95¢

THE DIVINE PITY
By Gerald Vann, O.P. D109—75¢

SPIRITUAL CANTICLE
*By St. John of the Cross
Translated, with an introduction
and notes, by E. Allison Peers*
D110—$1.45

THE WHITE FATHERS
By Glenn D. Kittler D111—95¢

SAINT AMONG SAVAGES:
*The Life of Isaac Jogues
By Francis Talbot, S.J.*
D112—$1.45

THE THIRD REVOLUTION:
*A Study of Psychiatry and Religion
By Karl Stern* D113—75¢

**WE HAVE BEEN FRIENDS
TOGETHER and ADVENTURES
IN GRACE**
By Raissa Maritain D114—$1.25

WE DIE STANDING UP
Dom Hubert van Zeller, O.S.B.
D115—65¢

STAGE OF FOOLS:
*A Novel of Sir Thomas More
By Charles A. Brady* D116—95¢

THIS IS ROME:
*A Pilgrimage in Words and Pic-
tures
Conducted by Fulton J. Sheen
Described by H. V. Morton
Photographed by Yousuf Karsh*
D117—95¢

**A WOMAN CLOTHED WITH THE
SUN**
Edited by John J. Delaney
D118—85¢

ST. AUGUSTINE OF HIPPO
By Hugh Pope, O.P. D119—$1.35

INTERIOR CASTLE
*By St. Teresa of Avila
Translated, with an introduction
and notes, by E. Allison Peers*
D120—75¢

THE GREATEST STORY EVER TOLD
By Fulton Oursler D121—95¢

THE MEANING OF MAN
By Jean Mouroux D122—85¢

WE AND OUR CHILDREN
By Mary Reed Newland D123—85¢

SOUL OF THE APOSTOLATE
*By Jean-Baptiste Chautard,
O.C.S.O.* D124—85¢

**CATHOLIC VIEWPOINT ON
CENSORSHIP**
By Harold C. Gardiner, S.J.
D125—75¢

THE SONG AT THE SCAFFOLD
By Gertrud von Le Fort D126—65¢